The Demonstration in
Pushkin Square

The Demonstration in Pushkin Square

*The Trial Records with Commentary
and an Open Letter*

by

PAVEL LITVINOV

TRANSLATED BY

Manya Harari

Gambit
INCORPORATED
Boston
1969

FIRST PRINTING

© in the English translation Harvill Press 1969
    in the Russian text Pavel Litvinov 1968
Library of Congress Catalog Card Number: 77–91996
Printed in the United States of America

Published in Great Britain by Harvill Press Ltd., London

Contents

CONTENTS

*Everyone has the right to freedom of peaceful
assembly and association.*

Universal Declaration of Human Rights, Article 20/1

INTRODUCTION

Introduction

There is a well-known children's tale in Russia about a carrot that a certain old man could not get out of the ground. He called his old woman to help him; Granny pulled Grandpapa, Grandpapa pulled the carrot, but they could not get it out. In the course of this very popular story more and more persons are called upon to help, and in the end they pull out the carrot. Explaining the course of events that led to the publishing of this book is somewhat like telling that Russian tale, with the difference that all those people together did not succeed in pulling the carrot out, but were themselves buried one after the other.

Two Russian writers, Sinyavsky and Daniel, using the pen names of Tertz and Arzhak, published in the West (1959–1965) a number of stories and an essay on socialist realism. They were arrested (September, 1965) and sentenced (February, 1966) to seven and five years' hard labor respectively. The 1954 youth sculling champion of the USSR, Alexander Ginzburg, who had already written a letter about the trial to Kosygin, compiled a White Book on the case, containing a transcript of the trial and many Soviet and foreign reactions. He sent copies of this typewritten book to Kosygin, to the KGB, and to several members of the Supreme Soviet. Ginzburg's associates, Galanskov, Dobrovolsky, Lashkova, and Radzievsky, were arrested on January 17–19, 1967. On January 22 a group of people demonstrated in Pushkin Square in Moscow, demanding freedom for those arrested. Their demonstration was broken up by the police and a number of demonstrators were arrested in their turn: this book is about their trials. Ginzburg himself was arrested the day after the demonstration and tried in February, 1968.

Now let us see where we have got to: this book is a collection of documents relating to the trial of Khaustov and Gabay (February, 1967) and the trial of Bukovsky, Delaunay, and Kushev (August–September, 1967), who had been arrested for demonstrating against the arrest of Galanskov, Dobrovolsky, Lashkova, and Radzievsky (of whom Radzievsky was later set free), who were arrested because they had helped Alexander Ginzburg (who was arrested on January 23, 1967, and tried, together with Galanskov, Lashkova, and Dobrovolsky, in February, 1968) to compile a White Book on the case of Sinyavsky and Daniel, who were sentenced to seven and five years' hard labor respectively (February, 1966) because they had published in the West, under the pen names of Tertz and Arzhak, in the years 1959–1965, a number of short stories and an essay on socialist realism.

Demonstrations not organized by the authorities are something new in the Soviet Union, where most citizens would not even dare walk the streets with a poster saying "Long live our glorious Communist Party!" unless they were told to do so. One should not think of these demonstrations as very spectacular events. There are hardly ever more than one, two, ten, twenty demonstrators, who assemble at a certain place (a foreign embassy, Pushkin Square, the *Lobnoye mesto* in Red Square) and at a given moment display small cardboard posters or banners. Banners can be rolled up and are easier to transport to the place of the demonstration, but it is not easy to find cloth for them. Cardboard posters are somewhat easier and cheaper to make, but are difficult to carry: since a demonstration may last only a few minutes before it is broken up by the police, posters cannot be carried openly to the place of the demonstration. They have to be wrapped in paper, and must be unwrapped at the right moment.

The demonstration of January 22 was not only against the arrest of Ginzburg's friends, but also against the introduction of Articles 190/1 and 190/3 into the Criminal Code of the RSFSR, which make the disturbance of public order and the spreading of slanderous inventions about the Soviet state and social system punishable offenses.

It is not quite clear what the Soviet government meant to achieve by quietly, almost secretly, introducing these articles. Disturbance of public order was already covered by Article 206 (hooliganism). Uttterances considered dangerous by the authorities could be dealt with under Article 70 (anti-Soviet agitation and propaganda).

3

An explanation could be that the government wanted legal means to handle undesirable public activities— regardless of what the political nature of such activities might be. To understand this need, one should realize that as a rule no public activity of any kind is tolerated unless initiated, organized, and controlled by the government. However, this control by the government is often masked: people attending the state funeral of a Soviet dignitary or taking part in a demonstration before a foreign embassy are supposed to be there spontaneously, of their own free will. This gives Soviet citizens grounds for regarding this freedom as *real,* and for holding demonstrations of their own.

One could reason along the same lines about Article 190/1: in the Soviet Union we have on the one hand a very stringent censorship of the printed word but, on the other hand, total silence about this censorship, and a freedom of the press guaranteed by the Constitution. Censorship does not even *exist* legally, which gives Soviet authors the possibility (in practice restricted, because they have no printing facilities at their disposal) of "publishing" manuscripts without the approval of the censor. It might be embarrassing to the authorities to have to rely solely on Articles 206 and 70 when prosecuting people for, say, distributing leaflets giving the text of the Declaration of the Rights of Man, or for openly canvassing for Tvardovsky as President of the Writers' Union.

The long and sordid story of the Soviet repression of freedom is sometimes enlivened by a touch of historic

4

irony. No public mention is ever made of Soviet censorship, because this is forbidden by the censors. In the spring of 1968, Western correspondents in Moscow were called to the Press Department of the Soviet Ministry of Foreign Affairs and warned that severe measures would be taken against them if they went on publishing news from unauthorized sources—news of this warning included. The demonstrators of January 22 were tried under the same Article 190/3 against which they had demonstrated.

The case for the defense was argued simply and convincingly. There had been no real disturbance of public order. Traffic, motorized or pedestrian, was not impeded. As to fighting and shouting, Bukovsky had—once—shouted "Down with dictatorship!" and Khaustov had initially resisted arrest. But the people arresting him had not identified themselves as volunteer guardians of the law, and could one speak of a disturbance of public order if one man had shouted two words in a public square? As to the placards, if the prosecution held them to be anti-Soviet, why then were the accused not tried under Article 70? Is asking for freedom for arrested friends and criticizing a new law to be considered disturbing the public order? Does not the Constitution of the USSR grant all citizens the freedom to demonstrate? Would it not be slandering the Constitution to imply that this freedom means only the freedom to demonstrate *for,* but not *against* the government?

The case for the prosecution was, as the reader will see, argued with less skill. Russia has always had a lack of talented defenders of the government against domestic criticism. Before the Revolution, men like Katkov and Pobedonostsev were the best the government could muster. The same goes for the Soviet Union today. The young men in the dock were not only wittier and braver, but also more intelligent and better versed in Soviet law than their prosecutors and judges.

It is true that the case for the prosecution was a difficult one. The prosecutor could, however, have argued that *any* organized group activities not controlled by the authorities were illegal—that, say, three boys starting a club of Pushkin readers without first consulting the authorities about such a move were punishable by law. He could have based this argument on the Soviet Constitution, which states clearly that the "leading nucleus" of every social organization in the USSR is the Communist Party. Anyone trying to form an organization, and, by implication, anyone trying to organize any kind of social activity without guidance from the Party, is thus acting against the Constitution and threatening the social structure of the country. In arguing these points clearly, however, the prosecution would have made it clear that no real freedom of demonstration, etc., does in fact exist in the Soviet Union—and this in itself would constitute an obvious case of anti-Soviet propaganda.

The defense had, for that matter, an analogous problem. A *real* defense in the normal, legal sense of the word would not only have aggravated the position of the defendants, but also would have endangered the lawyers personally. The defense had to identify itself with some of the points of view of the prosecution: it had to accept that Khaustov's doubts about the validity of Marxism-Leninism shed a poor light on his personality, that dreams about the British parliamentary system were necessarily "childish," and that what the defendants had done was wrong.

In a sense, neither the prosecution nor the defense could state the simple truth, obvious to all present: that the Soviet Union is a police state where no freedom of expression exists. The defense could avoid this issue by simply not referring to it. The prosecution and the court had to be careful to conduct the trial in such a way that the issue would not arise.

A few words about the author of this book: Pavel Mikhailovich Litvinov was born in Moscow in 1940. He is of mixed Jewish, Russian, and English stock. His grandfather, Maxim Maximovich Litvinov (1876–1951), was from 1930 to 1939 People's Commissar of Foreign Affairs (Foreign Minister) of the Soviet Union, and from 1941 to 1943 Ambassador to the United States. He studied physics in Moscow, was not always a brilliant student—from time to time he could be seen at the Moscow racetrack—and became a physics instructor at a Moscow institute of higher learning. Politically he grew up as a model citizen. As a boy he was a member of the Young Pioneers and, as he once told me, would have gladly attacked any boy speaking ill of the Great and Beloved Leader—a remark which broke the ice between us, since I, too, had once been a member of this organization and an admirer of the late Joseph Stalin. His difficulties in matters of faith seem to have begun with the trial of Daniel and Sinyavsky. He was mildly curious, went to have a look, but did not dare go near the court building. Wanting to know what these writers were tried for, he started to read their works. Being honest, he was struck by the gross injustice of sentencing writers to five and seven years of hard labor for a couple of stories and an essay on socialist realism, and he decided to join those who wanted to do something about it.

This "conversion" is typical of many Soviet intellectuals in the 1960's. It is an irony of history that while the Soviet authorities were jailing and killing completely innocent people by the hundreds of thousands, year after terrible year under Stalin, many Soviet intellectuals sincerely believed the victims to be guilty. As soon as the government began to prosecute people—as a rule—only for things they had actually done, and established something remotely resembling due process of law, it started losing the confidence of the intelligentsia at an astonishing rate.

This is, however, less amazing than it seems. In the years 1918–1953, famous writers were shot for being murderers, counterrevolutionary conspirators, terrorists, traitors, spies, fascist dogs, and the like. Now they are being sentenced to seven and five years' hard labor for writing satirical stories and essays. To the average Communist and fellow traveler, both in the West and in the Soviet Union, the former procedure was acceptable, the latter is not.

After the two trials of the demonstrators, Pavel Litvinov was called to the KGB headquarters and officially warned that he would be arrested and tried under Article 190/1 if a book such as the one he was working on should ever be made public. Litinov was not deterred by this warning. He made a transcript of his talk with the KGB officer and sent it to various newspapers. Eventually it was published in the West, and Litvinov's name became known to the millions of Soviet radio citizens who listen daily to the broadcasts in Russian of Western radio stations. He attached to his letter the text of Bukovsky's last plea, defying the KGB to arrest him by doing exactly the thing the KGB had warned him about. He completed his book in the spring of 1968. Copies of it began to circulate in Moscow, and one of the copies came into my possession. It is the English translation of this copy which is here presented to the English-speaking public.

In the course of 1968, Litvinov's signature was seen at the foot of various protest documents. The most famous of all is the "Appeal to world public opinion," signed by him and Daniel's wife Larisa, and distributed to foreign journalists during the Ginzburg-Galanskov trial. This was probably the first time in the history of the Soviet Union that two citizens of that country called openly upon their fellow citizens to raise their voices in protest against the government. He also signed a letter of protest against the arrest of Anatoly Marchenko, the author of *My Testimony,* an autobiographical account of six years spent in post-Stalin Soviet labor camps, shortly to appear in an English translation.

The trial of Marchenko (he was arrested for allegedly violating a passport regulation and sentenced to the maximum penalty for that offense: one year of forced labor) was held on August 21, 1968—the day of the invasion of Czechoslovakia. Marchenko's friends met that day in the courtroom (it was, for a change, a genuinely open trial), heard there about the invasion, and decided to hold a demonstration in Red Square on the following Sunday. Litvinov knew that the consequence of such a demonstration would be inevitable arrests and that the heavy sentences that would follow would considerably weaken the ranks of the dissidents in Moscow. When his friends nevertheless decided to go through with it, he joined them in Red Square, was beaten up, arrested, tried, and sentenced to five years' exile in Siberia. His address at present is USSR, Chitinskaya oblast, Tungokochensky rayon, Verkhnie Usugi, poste restante. Readers sending him a postcard can, if they so wish, give him greetings from his friend and admirer,

Karel van het Reve

April 1969

THE NEW DECREE AND
THE DEMONSTRATION

THE NEW DECREE AND THE DEMONSTRATION

On the 16th of September, 1966, the Presidium of the Supreme Soviet of the RSFSR[1] passed a Decree by which it added three new articles to the Criminal Code of the Republic, among them the following:

ARTICLE 190/1   The systematic dissemination by word of mouth of deliberately false statements derogatory to the Soviet state and social system, as also the preparation or dissemination of such statements in written, printed, or any other form, is punishable by three years of detention, or one year of corrective labor, or a fine up to one hundred rubles.

ARTICLE 190/3   The organization of, or active participation in, group activities involving a grave breach of public order, or clear disobedience to the legitimate demands of representatives of authority, or interference with the work of transport, state, or public institutions or services, is punishable by three years of detention, or one year of corrective labor, or a fine up to one hundred rubles.

The Decree was published only in the *Bulletin of the Supreme Soviet of the RSFSR* and not even mentioned in the rest of the Soviet press. A group of Soviet writers and other prominent citizens addressed the following letter to the authorities:

To the Supreme Soviet of the RSFSR
Copies to the Politbureau of the Central Committee of
       the CPSU
       the Presidium of the Supreme Soviet of the
       USSR
       the Prosecutor General of the USSR
Comrade Deputies,

As Soviet citizens we feel it our duty to bring to your notice our attitude toward the Decree passed by the Presidium of the Supreme Soviet of the RSFSR on the 16th of September, 1966.

In our view, the addition to the Criminal Code of Articles 190/1 and 190/3 opens the way to the subjective and arbitrary interpretation of any statement as deliberately false and derogatory to the Soviet state and social system.

We are convinced that these articles are contrary to the Leninist principles of socialist democracy and that, should the Decree be confirmed by the Supreme Soviet, they will form a potential obstacle to the exercise of liberties guaranteed by the Constitution of the USSR.

s. m. ANTONOVA, member of the CPSU since 1904

b. l. ASTAUROV, academician, cytologist

v. VOYNOVICH, writer

b. l. GINZBURG, academician, physicist

s. a. DAVYDOVSKAYA, member of the CPSU since 1925

yu. DOMBROVSKY, writer

ya. b. ZELDOVICH, academician, astro-physicist

d. yu. ZORINA, member of the CPSU since 1917

v. KAVERIN, writer

i. l. KNUNIANTZ, academician, chemist

m. a. LEONTOVICH, academician, physicist

a. b. MIGDAL, academician, physicist

v. NEKRASOV, writer

m. i. ROMM, film producer

a. d. SAKHAROV, academician, physicist

a. d. SKAZKIN, academician, historian

i. e. TAMM, academician, physicist

v. m. TUROK-POPOV, doctor of historical sciences

d. d. SHOSTAKOVICH, composer

p. i. YAKIR, historian

A. B. Volpin, Doctor of Physics and Mathematics, also wrote to the appropriate authorities, demanding a stricter formulation of Articles 190/1 and 3, on the grounds that they opened the way to the arbitrary interpretation of the lawful actions of Soviet citizens.

These letters remained unanswered. Academician Leontovich was told by the Central Committee of the

CPSU that the Decree was *not* intended to restrict the liberties of Soviet citizens.

At the end of December 1966 the Decree was confirmed by the Supreme Soviet of the RSFSR.

On the 17th–19th of January, 1967, four citizens— Galanskov, Dobrovolsky, Lashkova, and Radzievsky— were arrested. They were charged under Article 70 of the Criminal Code of the RSFSR (anti-Soviet agitation and propaganda).[2]

On the 22nd of January, at 6 P.M., a group of twenty to thirty young people gathered in Pushkin Square carrying posters calling for the release of the four prisoners and the revision of "the anti-constitutional Decree" of the 16th of September, and of Article 70 of the Criminal Code. The moment they displayed their posters, men in plain clothes rushed up from all sides of the Square, seized the posters, and arrested [3] several people. Most of the other demonstrators scattered, only a small group remained; one of these shouted: "Down with dictatorship! Release Dobrovolsky!" He, too, was arrested. All the prisoners were taken to the HQ of the Operational Squad of the Komsomol.[4] After several hours' questioning, two were released (Gabay and Delaunay) and two others (Kushev and Khaustov) taken to the KGB [5] investigation center at Lefortovo prison.

On the 25th and 26th of January, Gabay and Delaunay were re-arrested and another demonstrator, Bukovsky, was taken into custody. The houses of all the prisoners and of their friends and acquaintances were carefully searched; the police were particularly interested in so-called *samizdat*[6] (manuscripts) and confiscated most of them.

No less than a hundred witnesses were questioned by the Prosecutor's Office and the KGB.

On the 15th of February, it suddenly became known that two of the arrested demonstrators, Khaustov and Gabay, were to be tried on the following day.

TRIAL OF KHAUSTOV

SESSION OF THE MOSCOW CITY CRIMINAL COURT

16th of February, 1967

CHAIRMAN[7]: Panteleyeva
PEOPLE'S ASSESSORS: Mikhin and Biryukov
CLERK OF THE COURT: Fomicheva
PROSECUTOR: Starosvetov
COUNSELS: Kallistratova (defending Khaustov) and
Zharova (defending Gabay)

11 A.M.

The accused are brought in under guard: V. A. Khaustov (described in the indictment as 30, Russian, secondary education, unmarried, non-Party, worker in a wallpaper factory, no previous criminal record) and I. U. Gabay (42, Jew, higher education, non-Party, married, five-year-old son, editor of *Bulletin of Central Research Institute of Pedagogics,* no previous record). Both are charged under Article 190/3 and Khaustov also under Article 206/2[8] of the criminal code of the RSFSR.

PROSECUTOR: As the Moscow Prosecutor's Office has evidence of equally serious offenses previously committed by Gabay, and these require further investigation, I request that Gabay's case be handed to that office for further investigation.

ZHAROVA: I object. The Prosecutor's Office has handed over the case to this Court which should proceed on the evidence as at present before it.

KALLISTRATOVA: The law empowers the Court to reach its verdict on no more than the evidence before it. If the Prosecutor's Office has additional evidence, this should be submitted to the Court and both sides should have access to it before the hearing.

(After some deliberation, the Court grants the Prosecutor's request.) KALLISTRATOVA requests that the hearing of Khaustov's case be adjourned to a future date or the Court go into recess, as the defense has had no opportunity to consider the evidence.

The Court goes into recess until 2 P.M.

2 P.M.

KALLISTRATOVA requests a more thorough psychiatric examination of Khaustov than the one he underwent after his arrest. In 1964 Khaustov had been diagnosed as a schizophrenic. This is a highly complicated condition of which the diagnosis cannot be confirmed or refuted on the basis of a single interview with a psychiatrist. Khaustov's mother, who is in court, can give evidence that several of his close relations suffer from mental disorders.

JUDGE (to Khaustov): Do you agree to your counsel's request?

KHAUSTOV: No. I consider myself sane.

(After three minutes' deliberation, the Court refuses to grant the request on the grounds that it has no reason to doubt the report of the competent experts who pronounced Khaustov sane.)

JUDGE (reads out the Indictment): Khaustov, being a friend of Dobrovolsky, Galanskov, and others who had been arrested and charged under Article 70 of the Criminal Code of the RSFSR, has—in breach of the established procedure for making representations to the appropriate authorities—adopted the illegal course of furthering his demands by means of group activities involving a grave breach of public order, which took place in Pushkin Square at 6 P.M. on the 22nd of January. Khaustov and Gabay took active part in these proceedings, together with Kushev, Delaunay, and others. Khaustov informed his friends of the date and place of the demonstration and invited them to attend. Three banners were displayed, two of them with the slogan "Release Dobrovolsky, Galanskov, Lashkova, and Radzievsky" and another saying "We demand the revision of the anti-constitutional Decree and of Article 70 of the Criminal Code of the RSFSR." Khaustov disobeyed the orders of members of the Komsomol Operational Squad (Vesna and others), refused to give up his banner, and committed acts of malicious hooliganism: he tried to break free and pushed away the members of the

Komsomol who were holding him, struck Kleymenov on the shoulder and Vesna on the arm and leg, and used foul language. He thereby committed an additional grave breach of public order and is therefore charged under Article 206/2 as well as 190/3.

JUDGE: When were you informed of the charge?

KHAUSTOV: I don't remember exactly. Saturday, I think.

(Khaustov's signed receipt for the Indictment, dated the 11th of February, is produced.)

JUDGE: Do you understand the charge?

KHAUSTOV: Yes, I understand it.

JUDGE: Do you plead guilty?

KHAUSTOV: I plead guilty to only part of it.

JUDGE: Which part?

KHAUSTOV: I resisted arrest and may unintentionally have struck someone.

INTERROGATION OF WITNESSES

KLEYMENOV (the head of the Moscow Town Committee of the Komsomol and head of the Moscow Komsomol Operational Squad): On the 22nd of January, 1967, I and other members of the Squad were on duty in the Pushkin Square district. We met in the Square and were patrolling near the Pushkin statue and the Rossia Cinema. At 6 P.M. (I remember the exact time because I happened to light a cigarette and look at my watch) a group of some twenty to thirty young people gathered near the statue. I read the slogans [gives the texts] and was most astonished. I went up to the young people and asked what was going on. No one answered. I introduced myself and asked them to remove the banners. They did not comply. I took hold of one of the banners by the strip of material and tried to pull it down. Khaustov resisted. The man who had been holding one end of the banner dropped it and disappeared in the crowd, but Khaustov held on to his end, swinging the pole to and fro in front of my eyes, and striking me twice on the left shoulder. I closed with him and we struggled. Khaustov kicked out and tried to knock me off my feet. I seized him by the waist and grabbed his foot to keep him quiet but he went on kicking. By then two of my colleagues, Vesna and Bezobrazov, had joined me and Khaustov resisted them as well. They took him by the arms and led him to our HQ in Soviet Square. I accompanied them as far as Gorki Street and came back to the Square. During the struggle, I heard someone call out: "Don't resist the *Druzhinniki!*" [9] By the time I came back, the group near the monument had scattered but about ten minutes later it gathered again and a tall young man shouted: "Down with dictatorship! Release So-and-so!" I went up to him and asked him what he meant—who had been arrested and whom did he want released. He said they were his friends. I told him: "You'll have to come along with me and explain just what has been going on here." He came along. I found one of my colleagues near our car, told him to drive the young man to the HQ, and again returned to the Square. There was a girl among the group, whom I remembered from the 5th of December.[10] You know how it sometimes happens: you look at somebody and they look at you, and you recognize them at once. She was not arrested.

(The Prosecutor reminds him of his statements during the preliminary investigation and Kleymenov confirms them.)

KALLISTRATOVA: Were you wearing armbands?

KLEYMENOV: Some of us were, but not all.

KALLISTRATOVA: Did you have one on yourself?

KLEYMENOV: No.

KALLISTRATOVA: Do you believe that Khaustov struck you deliberately or by accident?

KLEYMENOV: We were both excited and telling each other to calm down. Several blows were struck. I believe he only struck two deliberately, and the rest by accident in the course of the struggle.

KALLISTRATOVA: Did he actually kick you?

KLEYMENOV: I'm an experienced *Druzhinnik* and it's not so easy to knock me down, but I felt that was what he was trying to do. And someone else kept pushing me from behind.

KALLISTRATOVA: Did you hear Khaustov swearing?

KLEYMENOV: I couldn't say whether he used bad language or not. I didn't put it in my report because I didn't actually hear it.

KALLISTRATOVA: Was it noisy in the Square? Was there a disturbance?

KLEYMENOV: On the whole it was quiet. There was just the one shout after Khaustov had been led away.

But Khaustov's resistance and the tussle we had with him were in themselves a breach of the peace.

VESNA (member of the Komsomol Operational Squad): As a member of the Squad, I was on duty in Pushkin Square. When I saw a group of citizens raising banners, I went up to Khaustov, who held one of them together with another citizen, and ordered them to put an end to this outrage. They refused.

JUDGE: What form did their refusal take?

VESNA: They ignored my order. After that, Bezobrazov and I took the banner away from them. Khaustov resisted; he swung the banner to and fro, hitting me twice on the arm and kicking out. We overpowered him and led him away.

JUDGE: Where did you take him?

VESNA: A comrade from Security was with us; he told us to take him to our HQ.

JUDGE: How did Khaustov behave on the way?

VESNA: He came quietly. We didn't even have to hold him.

JUDGE: Which way did you go? Through Gorki Street?

VESNA: No, through the back streets.

PROSECUTOR: Was Khaustov swearing?

VESNA: Yes, he was. He used foul language.

KALLISTRATOVA: What did he say?

VESNA shrugs his shoulders.

KALLISTRATOVA: I mean, was it obscene, unprintable language, or the kind in common use?

VESNA: It was unprintable. It is not in common use.

KALLISTRATOVA: Was he shouting obscenities and creating a disturbance?

VESNA: Khaustov swore once, not very loudly.

KALLISTRATOVA: Were people next to him bound to hear?

VESNA: Certainly.

KALLISTRATOVA: But if they were standing just a little farther away?

VESNA (unsure): They might.

KALLISTRATOVA: Did Khaustov hit you deliberately, or was it by accident?

VESNA: I think it was by accident.

KALLISTRATOVA: Who came up to him first, you or Kleymenov?

VESNA: First me, then Bezobrazov. I didn't see Kleymenov when I went up to Khaustov.

KALLISTRATOVA: Were you and Bezobrazov wearing armbands?

VESNA: I wasn't. I don't remember whether Bezobrazov was or not.

KALLISTRATOVA: What did you regard as a breach of public order?

VESNA: The fact that anti-Soviet slogans were displayed.

DVOSKIN (member of the Operational Squad): We were walking about the Pushkin Square district. A group of young people raised banners with anti-Soviet slogans.

JUDGE: What was written on the banners?

DVOSKIN quotes the slogans.

JUDGE: Were you patrolling the Square or the district?

DVOSKIN: The district. After the disturbances on the 5th of December we were told to keep an eye on the Square . . . Khaustov put up active resistance. He struck a member of the Squad in the face—afterward I heard it was Vesna. I think it was to push him away.

KALLISTRATOVA: You saw Khaustov arrested? Did those who arrested him wear armbands?

DVOSKIN: I saw our chaps go up to Khaustov. They asked him to come along with them to our HQ. So far as I could see, they were not wearing armbands.

KALLISTRATOVA: Did you introduce yourselves as *Druzhinniki?*

DVOSKIN: Yes.

KALLISTRATOVA: Did you, personally?

DVOSKIN: No.

KALLISTRATOVA: Did you hear anybody introduce himself to Khaustov?

DVOSKIN: According to our rules, we have to.

KALLISTRATOVA: During the preliminary investigation you gave evidence that Khaustov was fighting, now you state he was resisting.

DVOSKIN: If a man resists, it means he's fighting.

KALLISTRATOVA: But you have just said that he was simply pushing people back and trying to break free.

DVOSKIN: If a man is trying to break free and you let him, he'll fight.

KALLISTRATOVA: I see. All the same, could you be more exact—was Khaustov fighting or not?

DVOSKIN: Not in front of me, he wasn't. He was struggling and pushing people away.

KALLISTRATOVA: Did you, personally, hear Khaustov swearing obscenely?

DVOSKIN: No, I didn't. (Repeats his statement during the preliminary investigation, that he had not heard Khaustov use obscene language.)

KALLISTRATOVA: Where was Khaustov when you heard someone shout?

DVOSKIN: After Khaustov had been led away, I heard shouts of "Down with dictatorship!" and "Release Dobrovolsky!"

BEZOBRAZOV (student at Moscow Motor Road Institute and member of the Squad): Malakhov and I were walking along the Square from the direction of the Rossia Cinema. We approached a group of young people and saw banners. Some of our comrades had got there first and we saw Kleymenov and Vesna struggling with Khaustov. Khaustov struck Kleymenov on the back with a pole. I came to their assistance and we led him away.

JUDGE: How did he behave on the way?

BEZOBRAZOV: He was dragging his feet.

KALLISTRATOVA: Were you wearing an armband?

BEZOBRAZOV: Yes, I was.

JUDGE: Did the young people in Khaustov's group try to prevent your arresting him?

BEZOBRAZOV: They tried to keep us away from him. About four of them surrounded us.

KALLISTRATOVA: Did Khaustov use bad language?

BEZOBRAZOV: When he hit Kleymenov on the back, he used one or two unprintable expressions.

KALLISTRATOVA: You say Khaustov hit Kleymenov on the back but Kleymenov himself says that Khaustov hit him on the shoulder.

BEZOBRAZOV: It was when Kleymenov was dragging the banner down—he had his back turned to Khaustov and Khaustov hit him twice near the left shoulder. (Turns to show how this was done.)

MALAKHOV (member of the Squad): I was in command of five men. When I saw the slogans, I went up to a boy and girl who were holding one of the banners, introduced myself, and asked to see their identity papers. I took the banner away from them. Then we were surrounded, I was pushed away and lost sight of them. I was left holding the banner and young people from Khaustov's group took me for one of them and advised me to hide it and get away. I took it to the HQ. By then Khaustov had been brought there.

JUDGE: Had he been asked to show his identity papers?

MALAKHOV: Yes. He showed his reader's ticket.

KALLISTRATOVA: Did you hear him swearing?

MALAKHOV: No, I didn't. The boy and girl I talked to didn't swear. Whether Khaustov did or not, I couldn't say.

KALLISTRATOVA: Were you wearing an armband?

MALAKHOV: No, I was not.

CHERKASOV (member of the Squad): I was a fairly long way off from where it happened. I didn't see any fighting. I was standing behind some bushes and could only see the banners. Then a man was led past, about thirty yards from where I stood. He was hanging back.

JUDGE: Did you see his face?

CHERKASOV: It was dark and I was some way off. I couldn't make it out.

JUDGE: Do you know who it was?

CHERKASOV: No, I don't.

JUDGE: Do you know his name?

CHERKASOV says nothing, trying to remember.

JUDGE: If you can't remember, don't say anything. What happened after you saw him?

CHERKASOV: A group of people gathered and one of them shouted: "Down with the dictatorship of the proletariat! Down with dictatorship!" I went up and arrested Delaunay.

JUDGE asks him to be more definite about what was shouted.

CHERKASOV repeats what he said before and adds: The man who had been led away was dragging his feet all the time I saw him.

KALLISTRATOVA: Did you hear this man swearing?

CHERKASOV: He said something but there was too much noise for me to hear if he was swearing or not.

GRUZINOV (member of Special Police Squad).

JUDGE: Were you on duty?

GRUZINOV: Yes, we were patrolling.

JUDGE: Were were you in uniform?

GRUZINOV: Yes. Shcherbatov and I had just come on duty when a comrade in plain clothes came up and told us to arrest a comrade in a checked coat. I heard afterward that his name was Gabay. I took him to our car, he did not resist. Then we went back to the Square.

KALLISTRATOVA: Was there any shouting?

GRUZINOV: I didn't hear any.

KALLISTRATOVA: Did you see any disturbance in the Square?

GRUZINOV: No, there was no disturbance. Several citizens were standing about in groups near the statue. Everything was peaceful.

(At the end of each interrogation, the Judge asks Khaustov whether he wishes to question the witness. Each time Khaustov replies that he does not.)

INTERROGATION OF KHAUSTOV

KHAUSTOV: On the 20th of January I dropped in on my friend Galanskov and his father told me he had been arrested. I rang up Dobrovolsky and his wife said he had been arrested as well. I heard from other friends that Lashkova had been arrested too. After that I talked it over with my friends and we decided to hold a demonstration of protest.

JUDGE: Did you know what Galanskov had been arrested for?

KHAUSTOV: His father told me that, during the house

search, some papers had been confiscated including the periodical *Phoenix*.[11] I suggested to my friends that we should hold the demonstration near the Lenin Library, under the windows of the Presidium of the Supreme Soviet, but they didn't like the idea and in the end we decided to hold it in Pushkin Square. I rang up several other friends. We thought there would be about two hundred people but that evening was the opening night of a picture exhibition and most of them went there. We meant to have more banners as well, but in the end only three were made. I took part in making one of them. I fixed it to the poles, they were about 31.5 inches long. We were to display them at 6 P.M. and one of us— I won't disclose his name—was to make a statement about the arrests. If anyone came up and asked the reason for the demonstration, this same comrade was to explain. No one asked us to break up the demonstration. Instead, some people in plain clothes rushed up and immediately, without showing any credentials, tried to tear the banners away from us. They had no armbands. Kleymenov I know by sight—he was pointed out to me during the trial of Sinyavsky and Daniel: we didn't get into the courtroom but we were in the building and someone pointed him out to me and told me he was the head of the Komsomol Squad—but I did not see him on the 22nd in Pushkin Square. He was nowhere near me when I was arrested. The first thing they did was to twist my arms. I resisted and may, unintentionally, have hit someone, for which I apologize. I did not use obscene language.

34

JUDGE: You heard shouts of "Don't resist the *Druzhin-niki!*" Having heard this warning, why did you resist? Even if the method of arresting you was not correct, you ought to have submitted, and protested afterward through the proper channels.

KHAUSTOV: By the time I heard the shout we were in the middle of the struggle. They were twisting my arms, I was resisting, trying to keep my feet. I hadn't seen anyone in uniform or with an armband, I didn't at once realize what was going on and my instinctive reaction was to defend myself. It's possible that, in trying to break free, I hit someone accidentally. Once more, I apologize.

KALLISTRATOVA: Tell me, when you and your friends were planning the demonstration, was anything said about not creating a disturbance?

KHAUSTOV: Yes, we had a special talk about it. We agreed to be careful not to get in the way of the people in the Square or of the passers-by, not to go out into the roadway, not to block the footpaths, not to allow any noise or shouting. We agreed that we would submit to the demands of the police and the *Druzhinniki* and, when the demonstration was over, we would disperse quietly, without interfering with the traffic and using only the pedestrian crossings.

JUDGE: Did it occur to you that your activities might annoy other citizens?

KHAUSTOV: No, because we had no intention of creating a disturbance. If any citizen asked us what we were doing, we meant to explain.

JUDGE: Have you known Galanskov for long?

KHAUSTOV: Yes, two years.

JUDGE: Have you known Lashkova for long?

KHAUSTOV: I've met her but I don't know her well.

JUDGE: Have you known Dobrovolsky for long?

KHAUSTOV: Yes, I got to know him at the mental hospital.

JUDGE: Why were you there?

KHAUSTOV: For attempted suicide.

JUDGE: Did you tell Gabay there was to be a demonstration?

KHAUSTOV: No, not Gabay. I didn't know him.

JUDGE: You say you rang up your friends to arrange a meeting. During the preliminary investigation, Bukovsky gave evidence that he was rung up by a man who arranged to meet him because what he had to tell him could not be said over the telephone. Why didn't you give him the details over the telephone? Was it for reasons of secrecy or something else? Were you afraid the telephone was tapped?

KHAUSTOV: It would have meant a long conversation and would have taken too much time. It was simpler to talk things over when we met.

JUDGE: Do those whom you rang up share your opinions? Are they of the same way of thinking as yourself?

KHAUSTOV: We look at some things in the same way. I rang up my close friends, and they rang up people with a lot of friends.

JUDGE: Did you have any meetings to discuss the plans for the demonstration?

KHAUSTOV: Yes. We met at a friend's flat, but I won't disclose his name.

JUDGE: Did you go there by yourself or with someone else?

KHAUSTOV: I went with another friend, but I won't disclose his name either.

JUDGE: Then I'll put it to you plainly. Kushev has given evidence that you met at his flat and that you came with Bukovsky.

KHAUSTOV: Yes, that's true.

JUDGE: Who was to make the banners? Were you there when they were made?

KHAUSTOV: Yes, I was there. I won't tell you who made the banners, but I made the poles for one of them and fixed them on.

JUDGE: When your flat was searched, twenty-seven yards of white material were confiscated. Was that for banners?

KHAUSTOV: No. The banners were made of calico. That was staple fiber. I had to return it to the factory after finishing a job.

JUDGE: In your evidence during the preliminary investigation you said that your ideal society was the one described in Rousseau's *Social Contract*.

KHAUSTOV: No, I mentioned it only as an example.

JUDGE: In your evidence during the preliminary investigation you said that your ideal of government was the English parliamentary system. Is this still your view?

KHAUSTOV: Yes.

JUDGE: How much education have you had?

KHAUSTOV: Ten years' high school.

JUDGE: You did not go on to college?

KHAUSTOV: No. Last year I tried to join the Faculty of Philosophy at the University, but I failed the entrance exam.

JUDGE: In your evidence during the preliminary investigation you said that a technical college didn't interest you and you didn't want to go to an arts one because, there, your views would make things difficult for you. Why did you decide to try? Had you changed your views?

KHAUSTOV: I decided to make a closer study of Marxist philosophy.

JUDGE: Have you any knowledge of jurisprudence?

KHAUSTOV: No, but I was interested in the philosophy of law.

JUDGE: Which philosophers have you read?

KHAUSTOV: Kant. His books made me see a lot of things in a new light.

JUDGE: You would have been better advised to read something closer to our own time.

KALLISTRATOVA: Do you think you have studied Marxist-Leninist philosophy sufficiently deeply?

KHAUSTOV: I know it only superficially but enough, I think, to doubt the truth of its teaching.

JUDGE: Have you ever consulted anyone who knows it well?

KHAUSTOV: No, not really.

JUDGE: Why did you not choose some other form of protest? You could have written to the appropriate authorities.

KHAUSTOV: I was going to write a letter and collect a lot of signatures but, as the KGB stops all such attempts right from the start, I gave it up.

JUDGE: You did not write personally?

KHAUSTOV: No, I didn't.

JUDGE: What don't you like about Article 190?

KHAUSTOV: It abrogates liberties guaranteed by the Constitution.

JUDGE: Do you believe that all opinions should be freely expressed?

KHAUSTOV: Yes.

JUDGE: Whatever they are?

KHAUSTOV: Yes, because for every view there is an opposite one.

JUDGE: Do your friends also think that?

KHAUSTOV: Their opinions don't always coincide with mine.

JUDGE: Did you meet on purpose to discuss your views?

KHAUSTOV: We have known each other's views for years, we didn't have to meet on purpose for that.

JUDGE: Did you drink when you got together?

KHAUSTOV: Sometimes. But when we drank we didn't talk about our views.

JUDGE: Tell me, what sort of poles were the banners fixed to?

KHAUSTOV: They were about 31.5 inches long and half an inch across.

JUDGE: Actually, we don't need to have them described —let's have a look at them. (The banners are produced.) Are these the banners?

KHAUSTOV: Yes. That's the one I held with Delaunay.

PROSECUTOR: Are you sorry for what you did?

KHAUSTOV: No, I am not.

KALLISTRATOVA: Is there nothing you are sorry for?

KHAUSTOV: Only that I resisted arrest. Nothing else.

KALLISTRATOVA: Yet earlier, when you were questioned during the preliminary investigation, you pleaded guilty to malicious hooliganism.[12] Why did you?

KHAUSTOV: The interrogator told me that my resistance counted as malicious hooliganism. Afterward, when I thought it over and consulted my lawyer, I realized that I was guilty only of resisting but not of malicious hooliganism.

KALLISTRATOVA: Who are your parents?

KHAUSTOV: My father was killed in the war in 1944. My mother works in a factory.

JUDGE: The court has no more questions. Does the Prosecutor or Counsel for the Defense wish to make any request?

PROSECUTOR: No.

KALLISTRATOVA: I request permission to introduce, at a later stage, appeals for clemency, and evidence as to the character of the accused.

JUDGE grants the request.

SPEECH FOR THE PROSECUTION

Comrade Judges! This year is a great date for us—it is the 50th year of the Soviet regime. The struggle for the maintenance of public order continues throughout the country. In Moscow, the maintenance of public order is particularly important. We have largely been successful in this respect. Imagine, in the circumstances, the astonishment and indignation of the citizens who witnessed what occurred in Pushkin Square on the 22nd of January, 1967. The place which these self-styled demonstrators chose for their activities—the vicinity of a great poet's monument—is a place which everyone holds sacred. Their gathering might have attracted large crowds—not, of course, of like-minded citizens but of curious onlookers. Had the *Druzhinniki* not put a stop to it straight away, it might have led to a large disturbance.

Khaustov is both the organizer of this disturbance and an active participant. It is immaterial that he was no longer there when shouts were raised of "Down with dictatorship!" He organized the demonstration and, under Article 190/3, he bears the responsibility for everything that happened in the Square. He is also guilty of malicious hooliganism under Article 206/2. He resisted the *Druzhinniki*, he struck them, and he used obscene language. This is proved by the evidence of the witnesses. Counsel for the Defense raised the question of whether the *Druzhinniki* were wearing armbands; whether they did or not is irrelevant, because Article 206 covers resistance not only to representatives of authority or to *Druzhinniki* but to any citizens engaged in stopping acts of hooliganism. Whether he succeeded in inflicting bodily harm or not is equally immaterial.

It has no significance. We have heard his views here in court, and we know that he is a socially dangerous man. I deliberately asked him whether he regretted what he had done. He did not regret it. On these grounds I ask you to sentence Khaustov to two years' detention for malicious hooliganism under Article 206/2, and three years under Article 190/3, the two terms to run concurrently, and to be served in a corrective labor colony with a severe regime.[13]

KALLISTRATOVA requests that the hearing be adjourned to 10 A.M. on the following morning. She has been in court since 9 A.M. and is so tired that she feels unable to ensure an adequate defense.

The Court, after deliberating, announces a twenty-minute recess.

SPEECH FOR THE DEFENSE

I contest the charge, I contest the facts as stated in it, its definition of the crime, and its interpretation of Khaustov's actions. But even if I did not contest it, even if the Defense had no quarrel with the Indictment, I could still not accept, as proportionate to the offense, the severe penalty demanded by the Prosecution.

Khaustov is the son of a man who was killed in the war and of a woman who is a full-time factory worker. He is a worker himself. At twenty-eight, he has been working for ten years—all his adult life. Three years' detention—the penalty demanded by the Prosecution for Khaustov—is the maximum penalty under Article 190/3. This Article also provides for other and lesser penalties. The Court could impose a fine, or corrective labor without detention. The Prosecutor, however, bases his demand on the social danger of Khaustov's actions.

Article 37 of the Criminal Code requires the Court to take into account not only the offense but the character of the accused, and any aggravating or extenuating circumstances. In asking for the maximum penalty, the Prosecutor points out that Khaustov does not express regret. True, the law regards expression of regret as a mitigating circumstance. But the law has equally good reason not to regard failure to express regret as an aggravation of the offense.

We have seen Khaustov in court as a man of firm if misguided convictions, a man of difficult character but of staunch moral principles. He does not regard his actions, except resisting arrest, as criminal, and he has told the Court honestly about himself, as he did earlier, during the preliminary investigation. He has told the Court facts which it could not have known had he not revealed them. He has not tried to hide behind anyone's back, he has not lied, he has not evaded the issues, he has not attempted to mitigate his guilt by lies or evasion. He has refused to talk of what others have done, but the Court must not impute this to him as an aggravation of his guilt: his right to give or to withhold evidence is guaranteed by law.

Not one of the aggravating circumstances defined by

Article 37 has been claimed by the Prosecutor, yet he demands the maximum sentence.

The fact that Khaustov is a socially useful worker, that he has good references from his employers, that he has no criminal record—all these are extenuating circumstances under Article 37. I repeat, therefore, that even if I did not contest the facts as stated in the Indictment I would still have the right to ask for a milder sentence.

But I do contest the facts.

The Defense repudiates the charge of hooliganism. Khaustov is accused of using obscene language. Khaustov categorically denies this. During the preliminary investigation and the trial, he has shown himself to be a truthful man and, if he admits the other facts in the Indictment but categorically denies using obscene language, his evidence should be considered seriously as proof. And what has the Prosecution to set against it?

Witness Vesna states that Khaustov swore once, not very loudly. Witness Bezobrazov states that he swore once or twice, loud enough for people standing next to him to hear. But you, Comrade Judges, have established that in fact no one else heard him—not Kleymenov, not Dvoskin, not Malakhov, not Cherkasov. Who then heard this swearing? Whose ears were offended by it? Are we to believe Khaustov that he did not use obscene language? Are we to believe Vesna and Bezobrazov that he swore once or twice? In either case, this is not the public use of obscene language, not the intentional and insolent expression of disrespect for society defined by Article 206. Note that hooliganism is always a crime committed with intent. For a verdict under Article 206, it is clearly not sufficient to prove that, objectively, there has been a breach of public order (every crime is in some sense that). It must also be proved that the motive was hooliganism. But all the facts and circumstances in the case justify the Defense in asserting that Khaustov had no such motive, that his actions were dictated not by hooliganism but by something else. Apart from the unsubstantiated charge of swearing, Khaustov is accused of hooliganism on the grounds of refusing to comply with the legitimate demands of representatives of authority, and resisting arrest. The fact of his resistance[14] is admitted by Khaustov and the Defense does not deny it. But neither of these actions are hooliganism—they fall under Article 191, not 206, of the Criminal Code. Resistance can qualify as an aspect of hooliganism, but if there is no hooliganism, then resistance by itself does not justify a charge under Article 206.

In view of the Defense, Khaustov's physical resistance to arrest is an offense against Article 191, not against 191/1. We know from witnesses Kleymenov, Dvoskin, Vesna, and others that they wore no armbands. Bezobrazov is the only witness who states that he was wearing one. But you remember, Comrade Judges, that this armband was not noticed by Dvoskin. In that case, have we any reason to assume that Khaustov saw it? We know from witnesses Kleymenov, Bezobrazov, Vesna, and others that they called themselves, not *Druzhinniki,* but members of the Komsomol Operational Squad, so if Bezobrazov, before seizing Khaustov by the arms, did "introduce" himself, Khaustov could only regard him as an ordinary representative of the public. We have heard from Khaustov that it came as a surprise to him to be arrested in the absence of police in uniform or of men wearing armbands as *Druzhinniki*. Now, Article 191/1 applies expressly to resistance to police or to *Druzhinniki*. In the commentary on Article 191 it is stated specifically that members of the Komsomol patrols and operational squads are those representatives of the community to whom resistance is an offense under this article.

Neither does the Defense regard Khaustov's actions as an offense against Article 190/3. Khaustov is not a lawyer. He protested against Article 190/1 as anti-constitutional in the belief that it would make it possible for people to be prosecuted for expressing their ideas and opinions. We lawyers know perfectly well that our law does not admit of anyone being punished for his view of life, his thoughts, his ideas, however mistaken or harmful. The Prosecutor believes that Khaustov should be severely punished because his views are socially harmful. But under the law, no one can be punished for his views—this can only be done in disregard of the law. More than this, not all socially dangerous actions are punishable as crimes, but only those which are so defined by the Criminal Code. Both our Code and our legal practice have established that many socially dangerous actions, not directly covered by an article of the

Criminal Code, are not recognized as crimes and not therefore punished as such, but are dealt with by means of educational, social, and other pressures. This is why, whatever our social or political evaluation of Khaustov's actions, I maintain that he has not committed an offense punishable under Article 190/3 of the Criminal Code of the RSFSR.

No one, I think, can doubt that the offenses covered by this article are crimes committed with intent. Its provisions show that the intention must be to commit a serious breach of public order, to disobey representatives of authority, to disrupt the work of transport or other public institutions or services. We have seen from Khaustov's evidence that he had no such intention. In planning the demonstration he and the others who took part in it agreed among themselves that they would not obstruct pedestrians, not go out into the roadway, not make any noise, and that they would immediately submit should the police or the *Druzhinniki* intervene. There is nothing in the case to disprove this evidence. No other evidence of intent has been obtained by the Prosecution or the Court. We must therefore conclude that there was no intent to commit the offense provided for by Article 190/3. I have reason to maintain that, in actual fact, the group activities of Khaustov and his friends involved no breach of the peace. The group which gathered near the statue made no noise, created no disturbance: as you will remember, Comrade Judges, Kleymenov showed that everything was peaceful in the Square and that someone shouted only after Khaustov had been removed.

Khaustov cannot be accused of disobeying the authorities, because all the evidence goes to show that there were no representatives of authority in the Square. The police arrived after Khaustov had been arrested and in their evidence they say nothing about any act of disobedience. Witness Vesna of the Komsomol has told the Court that a breach of the peace was committed by a display of "anti-Soviet" slogans. There is no need for me to prove that the slogans were not anti-Soviet, since the term has not been used in the Indictment or the speech for the Prosecution.

A breach of public order was indeed committed, but not by the young people as a group: it was committed only by Khaustov in that he resisted members of the Komsomol Operational Squad. As I have already said, this is an offense against Article 191 but not against Article 190/3. This is why the Defense believes that Khaustov cannot be prosecuted under Article 190/3. If his views are wrong and harmful, Khaustov cannot be imprisoned for that. He must be slowly and patiently re-educated, he must be helped to rid himself of his childish ideas about Rousseau and the English parliament as the ideal social order. Education, not prison, will cure him of this sickness.

I ask the Court to dismiss the charge of obscene language and to find that Khaustov's resistance to arrest is an offense under Article 191, but not under Article 206, of the Criminal Code of the RSFSR. I ask the court to find him innocent under Article 190/3 and to impose a penalty, not involving detention, within the limits prescribed by Article 191.

KHAUSTOV'S FINAL STATEMENT

I am sorry that I resisted arrest and once again apologize to those who arrested me. I hope the verdict of the Court will be just.

VERDICT AND SENTENCE

(For full text, see Appendix I.)

Khaustov was found guilty on all counts and sentenced to three years' hard labor in a camp with a "severe" regime.

His Defense Counsel appealed to the Supreme Court of the RSFSR, which heard the appeal on the 31st of March and reduced the sentence to one of three years' hard labor in a camp with an "ordinary" (not a "severe") regime. (For full text of Supreme Court's verdict, see Appendix II.)

LETTER FROM GALINA GABAY

To the Chairman of the Presidium of the Supreme Soviet of the USSR.
Comrade Chairman,

I wish to inform you of what took place at the Moscow City Court on the 15th of February, 1967.

On the 15th of February, 1967, the cases of my husband, I. Gabay, and V. Khaustov—both arrested for their part in a demonstration near the Pushkin statue on the 22nd of January—came up for hearing at the Moscow City Court.

The day before, I went to the offices of the City Court to ask when the trial was to take place, as I wished to inform my husband's counsel. The official on duty told me that the date had not yet been fixed. On the same day, however, Advocate Zharova—appointed, under Article 49 of the Procedural Code, to defend my husband—informed me that the hearing was to start at 10 A.M. the following day (the 15th of February); she added that I would not be admitted to the courtroom. In a later conversation she told me that I could, after all, attend the hearing but begged me to bring no one else. She explained that no one was obliged to tell me the date of the hearing and it could perfectly well be held without me.

Next day I went at 9 A.M. but the police on duty at the entrance of the building were keeping everyone out. I knew that Judge Panteleyeva had no objection to my being present at the trial, yet it was only by a miracle that my mother-in-law and I managed to get into the courtroom, as the police and guards outside the door were keeping out everyone, including families and friends of the accused.

What was even more outrageous, a few minutes be-

fore the start of the trial a group of young men, who
were not relations, friends, or even acquaintances of the
accused, arrived and were let in at once without a single
question being asked. Equally promptly and silently,
their coats and hats were taken from them by the cloak-
room attendants who had at first refused to accept ours.

Obviously, the whole thing had been carefully pre-
arranged. The trial was officially described as a "hearing
in open court" and the "public"—consisting of these
young men—was there. After the recess, the same well-
organized group tried to push the rest of us—friends
and relations of the accused—away from the courtroom
door and did it so roughly that the Judge felt obliged
to say: "Let the mother in, it doesn't look well." With
the help of my friends, I managed to follow my mother-
in-law inside, but all the seats were taken so that she
and I had to stand until the recess when the young men
went out for a smoke.

To the best of my knowledge, a hearing in open court
is one which any citizen of our country—not to mention
relations and friends—has the right to attend. Any deliberate restriction of this right is intolerable.

Yet what is happening now? Why are families not
informed in advance of the date and time of the hearing? Why is this done only six or seven hours before
it begins? Why are they pressed to bring no one with
them, however close to the accused? And why are complete strangers allowed to jump the queue and go in
before the hearing, while friends and relations are kept
out?

My husband's case has been separated from Khaustov's and referred back to the Prosecutor's Office for further investigation.

Frankly, I am afraid that when his trial does come up, there will be just such another farce of an "open" judicial investigation.

I insist that when my husband's case is heard, the first to be admitted to the courtroom should be his family, relations, and friends—not people specially chosen to act the role of public.

GALINA GABAY
Teacher at the Moscow Correspondence
School for the Deaf

REPLY

To: Citizenness G. Gabay
    18 Novolesnaya Street, Block 2, Flat 83
    Moscow
From: Moscow Prosecutor's Office

Your complaint to Chairman of the Presidium of the Supreme Soviet, Comrade Podgorny, has been duly examined by the Moscow Prosecutor's Office.

On checking the facts it has been established that the trial of V. Khaustov and I. Gabay at the Moscow Court on the 15th of February, 1967, was conducted publicly, in full conformity with Article 18 of the Procedural Code of Criminal Law of the RSFSR.

Your complaint is therefore dismissed as groundless.

D. LEBEDEV

Deputy Head of Dep. for Control of
Criminal Trials, Junior Legal Counsel

OUTSIDE THE COURTROOM

Galina Gabay's letter gives a truthful account of the atmosphere inside the court building during Khaustov's trial.

Several details can be added. A hefty young man stood outside the courtroom and pushed the women roughly away from the door, while the police stood by and did nothing. When outraged members of the public demanded that he should apologize and disclose his identity, the police immediately let him into the courtroom. When those who were left outside the door insisted on going in as well and asked who the hooligan was, the police replied that all the seats were taken, the citizen's identity was unknown to them, they did not propose to check it, the real hooligans were those who wanted to go in and it was their identity that ought to be checked.

This man of unknown profession was one of dozens in and around the courtroom: some attended the trial in the role of the public; others blocked the door to the few friends and relatives of the accused (a dozen at most, since very few had heard of the trial in time to come); still others circulated in the building, listened to what people were saying and, after the trial, followed them home (naturally, at a respectful distance).

We know that much the same thing happened at the trial of Sinyavsky and Daniel in February 1966, at that of Bukovsky, Delaunay, and Kushev and, according to eyewitnesses, at several others.

All this should be kept in mind in considering the verdict which begins with the words: "The case was heard in open session."

There is a curious detail in the reply from the Prosecutor's Office. In her own letter, Galina Gabay had mistakenly given the date of the trial as the 15th of February, not the 16th. How thoroughly Junior Counsel Lebedev checked the facts to which she had referred is unknown, but the same mistake occurs in his reply.

RIGHTS OF THE ACCUSED

Article 2/1 of the Universal Declaration of Human Rights:
Everyone charged with a penal offense has the right to be presumed innocent until proved guilty according to law in a public trial at which he has all the guarantees necessary for his defense.

Article 3 of the Constitution of the USSR:
All Court hearings in the USSR are open, except in certain cases specified by law, and the right of the accused to defend himself is guaranteed.

Article 18 of the Procedural Code of Criminal Law of the RSFSR:

All Court sessions are open except where this would endanger a State secret.

Cases may also be tried in camera, if the Court so decides, where the accused is under sixteen years of age, or where it is held undesirable to publicize facts concerning the private lives of those involved in the case. The verdict must in all cases be announced publicly.

AFTER THE TRIAL

After the trial, the investigation of the cases of the other demonstrators went on: house searches, interrogation of accused, of witnesses, etc. It was conducted by Investigators Akimova and Gnedkovskaya of the Moscow Prosecutor's Office. In the course of the interrogations, intimate facts, real or alleged, from the lives of the accused, the witnesses, their friends and others, were widely discussed. The family of one of the accused were told by Investigator Akimova that he was in the habit of seducing minors. A number of questions were asked concerning another, worded in such a way as to create the impression that he was a sexual pervert. Extracts from a young girl's diary, confiscated during the search of her house, were read to many witnesses. These were only some of the attempts made to destroy the reputation of the accused and their friends.

In February, students of Moscow University began to

collect signatures for a letter of protest against the arrest of the demonstrators. The girl student who kept the text was followed by KGB agents, arrested on University premises, threatened with a house search, and forced to give up the letter. Several other attempts to protest are known to have been stopped in the same way.

In April the investigation was suddenly taken over by the KGB.

In June Gabay was released and in August his case was dismissed for lack of evidence. The only thing against him had been his *presence* in the Square at the time of the demonstration: he had taken no part in it. He had neither planned it nor carried a banner, neither shouted nor resisted arrest. Nevertheless he was kept in prison for four months.

Finally, the investigation was closed and the trial of Bukovsky, Delaunay, and Kushev began on the 30th of August.

TRIAL OF
BUKOVSKY, DELAUNAY,
AND KUSHEV

MOSCOW CITY CRIMINAL COURT

30th of August to 1st of September, 1967

CHAIRMAN: Yu. B. Shapovalova
PEOPLE'S ASSESSORS: P. D. Elfimov and L. N. Kireyeva
PROSECUTOR: V. M. Mironov
DEFENSE COUNSELS: D. I. Kaminskaya (defending Bukovsky), N. S. Alsky (defending Kushev), and Sh. A. Melamed (defending Delaunay)

N.B. The report omits certain procedural details, as when witnesses were warned of their legal obligation to give truthful evidence.

INDICTMENT

30th of August, 10 A.M.
V. K. Bukovsky (24, born in the city of Belebey in the Bashkir Republic, Russian, non-Party, unmarried, secondary education, unemployed, 3rd category disabled,

residing at 3/5 Furmanov Street, Flat 59, Moscow); V. N. Delaunay (19, born in Moscow, Russian, non-Party, secondary education, unmarried, freelance correspondent of *Literary Gazette*, residing at 12 Pyatnitskaya Street, Flat 5, Moscow); and Ye. I. Kushev (20, born in Odessa, Russian, non-Party, unfinished secondary education, unemployed at the time of arrest, residing at 10 Smolenskaya Street, Flat 174, Moscow), are all three charged under Article 190/3 of the Criminal Code of the RSFSR.

On the 17th of January, 1967, Galanskov, Dobrovolsky, Lashkova, and Radzievsky were arrested by the security police, and charged under Article 70/1 of the Criminal Code of the RSFSR. Among their friends who, in varying degrees, shared their views, were Bukovsky, Delaunay, Kushev, and Khaustov (since convicted). Acting as a group with other, so far unidentified persons, these men committed a serious breach of public order in Pushkin Square at 6 P.M. on the 22nd of January, 1967.

Bukovsky, an opponent of communist ideology, was first arrested in 1962 and charged under Article 70/1 for circulating anti-Soviet documents including photostats of part of Djilas's book *The New Class*. He was found mentally ill and sent for treatment to a mental hospital. Discharged in 1964, he got in touch with Tarsis and, through him, with representatives of the NTS,[15] to whom he and his friends (Batshev and Gubanov) handed typescripts of poems by young poets belonging to the so-called SMOG group.[16] In the summer of 1966 Bukovsky, jointly with Dobrovolsky, Gubanov, Delaunay, and Kaplan, repeatedly met an emissary of the NTS known as Philip, but no subversive actions on his part followed from these encounters.

Delaunay, left to his own devices since childhood, came under the influence of tendentious rumors concerning home and foreign policy (especially during the period of the Cult of Personality[17]). His interest in literature led him to attend gatherings in Mayakovsky Square where he established friendly relations with members of the SMOG group, including Gubanov, Dobrovolsky, Lashkova, Vishnevskaya, and others. This resulted in his writing the politically harmful *Ballad of Unbelief* of which he handed a copy to the emissary of the NTS known as Philip. There is, however, no available evidence of its publication abroad.

Kushev fell under the influence of the religious fanatic A. Levitin (Krasnov), became imbued with ideas of Christian Democracy, and adopted its viewpoint in regard to Soviet life. Evincing a morbid interest in every sort of anti-Soviet literature, he received, in the summer of 1966, from Kolosov (deceased), one copy of the periodical *Bell*,[18] produced and circulated by an anti-Soviet organization in Leningrad, and from Dobrovolsky, Katz, and Lashkova three NTS pamphlets entitled *The Power of Ideas, Solidarism—The Idea of the Future* and *Our Time,* which he read and returned to them.

Hearing of the arrest of their friends and wishing to draw public attention to it, Bukovsky and Khaustov (since convicted) organized a demonstration in Pushkin Square; three banners were prepared on their instructions, with the slogans "Release Dobrovolsky, Galanskov, Lashkova, and Radzievsky" and "We demand the revision of the anti-constitutional Decree and of Article 70"; Bukovsky and Khaustov notified their friends, explained the object of the demonstration, and invited them to attend. For this purpose, they called on Kushev and others. On the 22nd of January a group of some thirty people met in Bukovsky's flat and thence proceeded to Pushkin Square, one of the banners being carried by Delaunay, who hid it under his coat. The group assembled near the poet's monument at 6 P.M. and unfurled their banners. One was held by Khaustov and Delaunay, another by an unidentified young man and girl in dark clothes. *Druzhinniki* broke up the demonstration. Khaustov resisted. The group near the monument split into smaller groups. After a time, Kushev arrived in the Square, stood near one of these smaller groups, and shouted "Release Dobrovolsky! Down with dictatorship!"

Bukovsky, who had organized the demonstration and taken an active part in it, thereby committing a breach of the peace, pleaded not guilty, explaining that he had acted in protest against the arrest of his friends: "Hearing of the arrest of my friends, I decided to protest against this and to organize a demonstration. I informed my acquaintances and explained the object of the demonstration."

Delaunay, who took an active part in the breach of public order committed by the group, pleaded guilty, showed sincere repentance, and gave honest, truthful evidence: "I realized that the plan was absurd but, when Bukovsky said it was too late to go back, we must stick together, I was at a loss as to what to do; I decided to stick to my comrades and join the demonstration—I realize that this was a false idea of comradeship."

Kushev also took an active part in the activities of the group and has pleaded guilty. He reached the Square after the banners had been removed but, wishing to make some gesture in front of the gathering, shouted "Release Dobrovolsky! Down with dictatorship!" He said in his evidence: "Hearing of the demonstration, I could not stay away and decided to join it. I arrived late and went up to a group which included my friends Delaunay and Maslova, and a number of others whom I knew only by sight from having seen them with other friends."

(All three are charged under Article 190/3. For full text of charge, see Appendix III.)

INTERROGATION OF THE ACCUSED

DELAUNAY takes the stand.

JUDGE: Accused Delaunay, will you give evidence on the facts of the case and tell us what you can about yourself.

DELAUNAY: I was born on the 22nd of December, 1947. After my parents' divorce, I lived with my mother and younger brother. I was always very interested in the humanities—philosophy, history, literature—and began myself to write verse and prose at the age of thirteen.

Just at that time, in 1960, young poets and writers began to give readings in Mayakovsky Square. Today some of them have an established reputation. I often went to hear the poets of the so-called First Mayakovsky group, though I was too young to read my own work. It was in Mayakovsky Square that I first met the poet and journalist Yuri Galanskov and many others, though I only got to know them much later. I finished school externally and joined the Arts Faculty of the Lenin Teachers Training Course. I went to evening classes and, after passing an exam, was transferred to the day section. By then, from being interested in poetry as an amateur, I had come to see it as my vocation. I got in touch with SMOG—the most interesting group of young poets in Moscow. I should like to explain a little about them. SMOG was in a sense a revival of the "Mayakovsky group." The point is that the first group of that name had ceased to exist in 1963. The gatherings in Mayakovsky Square were broken up by the Komsomol Operational Squads and had to be discontinued. SMOG revived the tradition as early as the winter of '65–'66, reciting their poetry in Mayakovsky Square as well as before student audiences. They regarded Pasternak, Mandelshtam, and Tsvetayeva as their teachers and took up the cause of artistic freedom—freedom of form as well as of content. Their gatherings brought them into conflict with official bodies such as the Komsomol. Their conduct was, of course, not always right and often frivolous. I am thinking, for instance, of the time they held a demonstration near the writers' club with the slogan

"Socialist Realism must lose its Virginity." But neither
did the Komsomol or the Writers' Union,[19] to put it
mildly, take the right line. They forgot that they were
dealing with creative young people, writers, artists—I
would even venture to say, with the most gifted section
of our creative youth; instead of going into the facts,
they condemned them out of hand. What I am saying,
by the way, is nothing new. Sholokhov, in his address
to the Writers' Congress, spoke at length of the difficult, abnormal situation of a group of young writers
and said in so many words that it was not all their own
fault—the responsibility lay also with the Komsomol,
the Writers' Union, and other official organizations. I
was never myself a member of SMOG, though I took
part in some of their gatherings; my only reason for not
joining them officially was that their program seemed
to me too provocative, their behavior frivolous, and
their futuristic tendencies repelled me. Rejected by the
authorities, they began, in the summer of '66, to talk
about reciting poetry in the town squares again. It was
then that their leader Gubanov and I had the idea of
a new, legal organization on the same basis as SMOG
but with a much more serious, considered program.
This would avoid undesirable excesses while providing
facilities for fruitful discussion. It would also create
normal working conditions for young poets, writers,
and artists of the so-called Leftist trend. In the autumn
of 1966, I got to know Vladimir Bukovsky, who at once
warmly took up the idea. We talked it over at great
length and decided to found a discussion club as a basis

for an organization of young poets, writers, and artists who did not belong to any of our official literary or artistic associations. The nucleus was to be formed by those who had given readings in Mayakovsky Square in the early sixties, members of SMOG, and Leftists connected with both groups. Some well-known writers agreed to work with us and direct some of the groups. My friends from the young scientists' council of the Komsomol Town Committee advised me to go straight to the leaders of the Committee for help, and this we did. We submitted a proposal for a discussion group and a youth organization to be formed within the Komsomol in September, 1966. We asked the two Secretaries, Trushin and Rogov, to help us start the club and take part in its activities. At first the Komsomol received us with open arms. They were obviously sick of the incidents in the squares. We not only discussed the plan in theory, we submitted a draft constitution drawn up by Bukovsky and myself. We came to an agreement, though it was not quite finalized, to call a youth conference, and the Komsomol promised to provide the premises and to take part in it. It was fixed for the 16th of September. We were preparing for it and had already written to our friends in Leningrad and Kiev and asked several prominent writers as guests when, for reasons which were never explained to us, the Komsomol Town Committee suddenly refused to grant us the facilities it had promised, or indeed to cooperate in any way, thereby placing us in an extremely awkward position as this was only two days before the conference and we had the utmost difficulty in letting those we had invited know that it had been canceled. All the same, we accepted the decision. We didn't hold the conference illegally, although we could have done this, just because we wanted once again to prove our good intentions, to show that there was nothing subversive about our plans. After the refusal of the Town Committee to cooperate, we somehow felt like outcasts. Many of us even felt resentful. True, we didn't all lose hope of a rational solution of this painful and long-standing problem. Bukovsky, for one, applied to the Lenin Regional Committee of the Komsomol, and I myself took the matter right up to the Ideological Commission of the Party Central Committee. But it is no part of the functions of the Ideological Commission of the Party to start youth clubs or artistic associations, or to provide premises for conferences. Although Comrade Galanov, whom I saw, seemed interested in our plans and even asked to see a selection of our poems, somehow nothing ever came of it. Perhaps the Commission was too busy, perhaps it would have helped us in the end. But at the time, after our failure with the Town Committee of the Komsomol, the delay was discouraging. It was the same with the Regional Committee of the Komsomol where Bukovsky had left a small selection of our writings—we never got a definite answer. Meanwhile, the authorities at my college got to know of my disreputable connection with SMOG and my efforts to start an organization of writers. Evidently nervous about getting into trouble, they hastened to get rid of me, seizing on the pretext of my irregular attendance, although I had a doctor's certificate showing that I needed sick leave. At the same time, and in reality because of the same fears, I was expelled from the Komsomol. I broke down and had to go to a mental hospital. Perhaps I did brood too much on the situation—but the fact was that I had gone to the authorities for help with a perfectly sensible proposal, only to be thrown out of both my college and the Komsomol. In general I felt at the time as though nothing could go right for me.

But to come to the facts of the case.

On the 22nd of January my friends Bukovsky and Viktor Khaustov came to see me. They told me that Galanskov, Dobrovolsky, Lashkova, and Radzievsky, all of whom I knew, had been arrested and charged under Article 70 for producing the literary periodical *Phoenix*. The news positively shattered me—the more so because I felt to some extent at fault. After all, Bukovsky was to have been one of the founders of our organization, and Dobrovolsky and Lashkova had given us some purely practical help. I believed then, as I do now, that there would not have been a *Phoenix* incident if the Komsomol had not refused to help us. It was I who had conducted most of the negotiations, first with the Town Committee of the Komsomol, then with the Central Committee of the Party. I was to blame for failing to convince them of the need for an organization of artists and writers, and Galanskov and the others would now have to pay the price. Radzievsky too was on my conscience, since I had introduced him to my friends.

Bukovsky and Khaustov told me that a demonstration would be held in Pushkin Square to protest against the arrests and demand the revision of the anti-constitutional Articles 70 and 190. Bukovsky asked me if I was in sympathy with these aims and I said yes, because I knew that the Soviet Union had signed the Declaration of Human Rights and that one of them was the right to free expression of opinion by any means and across State frontiers, on the condition only that it did not incite to racialism or to war. This is why I did not believe that publishing something in the West was in itself a crime. As for *Phoenix,* I had heard enough about it to be sure that there could not be anti-Soviet propaganda in it. I had also read the text of Article 190. I believed that one should protest against it and I knew that the Supreme Soviet had in fact already received a protest.

Neither Khaustov nor Bukovsky told me that they themselves were the organizers of the demonstration. After they had left, I began to have doubts as to whether it was opportune or could serve a useful purpose. After all, we didn't really know what exactly Galanskov and the others had been arrested for, we could only guess at the reason. So perhaps, to say the least, we were being hasty. As my doubts grew and grew, I decided to ask the advice of someone who knew the law better than I did, and the next day (the 21st) I went to see Peter Ionovich Yakir; Kucherova came with me. There, we found Ilya Gabay who already knew about the demonstration. Yakir was against it. He said it was not only premature but could achieve nothing and was pointless. He asked me if it could still be stopped. I said I thought we must talk to Bukovsky so we all arranged to meet the following day at the Kropotkin Underground Station and from there go on to Bukovsky's flat. He said it was too late. Two of the banners were not being made at his flat and would be taken straight to the Square. That was that and there was nothing more to be said. Meanwhile the flat was filling with people, most of them strangers to me—I only knew Viktor Khaustov and Alexander Yesenin-Volpin. Yakir was still trying to dissuade me from going to Pushkin Square. I said that, though in principle I was against the demonstration, it was too late to talk about it now—for one thing, I'd feel too much of a fool if I left Bukovsky's flat, and anyway, I could simply not desert my friend at such a moment. Yakir and Gabay left. Yakir did not attend the demonstration. All of us at Bukovsky's talked about whether we would be committing an offense under Article 190, and we all came to the same conclusion—that we would not, unless we blocked the traffic or refused to obey representatives of authority. Bukovsky warned us each and all again and again of how important it was to obey the authorities and not do anything that would involve a breach of the peace.

PEOPLE'S ASSESSOR: Why did you want to form your own organization instead of joining one of the existing literary unions?

DELAUNAY: Most of them are affiliated with some factory or other institution.[20] What we had in mind was an organization on a city-wide—perhaps even a country-wide—scale.

PROSECUTOR: What makes you think that the reason you were expelled from college was your connection with SMOG?

DELAUNAY: It all happened so quickly, they expelled me without even giving me the chance to explain.

KUSHEV takes the stand.

JUDGE: Will you speak about the facts of the case.

KUSHEV: I heard about the demonstration from Bukovsky and Khaustov and I promised to come. I don't regard my arrested friends as criminals, and friendship matters to me more than points of law. I know Yuri Galanskov and Alexei Dobrovolsky (from the club and so on); I know they are decent people and I don't believe they could commit a crime. I decided to take part in the demonstration, not just be an onlooker—that is why I shouted the first two slogans that came to my mind.

PROSECUTOR: Do you believe in God?

KUSHEV: I have my own attitude to religion.

PROSECUTOR: Can you be more definite?

KUSHEV: Yes, I believe in God.

PROSECUTOR: Why is it that for a long time you were not doing any socially useful work?

KUSHEV: I was studying.

PROSECUTOR: You went to night school, you are supposed to have a job while you are there.

KUSHEV: I did from time to time—I could not stay long

in the same job because of my health. In any case, I was always busy. I am not a social parasite.[21]

PROSECUTOR: Did you realize that the demonstration was illegal?

KUSHEV: Article 125 of the Constitution allows demonstrations to be held in our country. Bukovsky said it was legal, and I have always thought myself that it was natural for citizens to show their feelings by demonstrating.

PROSECUTOR: Do you realize what you have done?

KUSHEV: It was thoughtless of me to shout, perhaps it was wrong, but I don't regard it as a breach of the peace.

BUKOVSKY: So far as you could see, was there any breach of the peace in the Square?

KUSHEV: No, there was not.

BUKOVSKY: What instructions did I give the demonstrators?

KUSHEV: You said there was to be no resistance, no shouting, no one must run out into the roadway, and we must ourselves prevent any attempt at creating a disturbance.

ALSKY (Kushev's Defense Counsel): Do you write poetry?

KUSHEV: Yes, but I don't consider myself a poet.

BUKOVSKY takes the stand.

JUDGE: Will you speak about the facts of the case.

BUKOVSKY: It was in 1961 that I first asked myself whether in fact the democratic liberties guaranteed by the Constitution are a reality in the Soviet Union.

JUDGE: Why 1961? What happened then?

BUKOVSKY: That was the year my friends Osipov, Kuznetsov, and Bokstein were tried as criminals for producing a handwritten periodical. This was unjust, and ever since I have been opposed to the atmosphere of oppression and concealment which exists in our country.

JUDGE: Today we are not discussing the actions of your friends but what you did yourself. Keep to the facts.

BUKOVSKY: I am. The arrest of Galanskov and the others was another such case. There are any number of them in our country—take, for instance, the trial of Sinyavsky and Daniel.

JUDGE: We are not talking about Sinyavsky and Daniel, we are talking about you.

BUKOVSKY: I request that, in accordance with Article 243 of the Procedural Code of Criminal Law of the RSFSR, it should be entered in the record that the Judge is not letting me have my say.

As an opponent of all forms of totalitarianism, I have made it my aim in life to denounce the anti-democratic laws which lead to political inequality in our country. I am against the recently adopted Decree because it contradicts the basic democratic liberties guaranteed by the Constitution. Demonstrations such as the one I organized are, in my view, a legitimate form of protest and of struggle for the abolition of such anti-democratic laws. Article 125 of the Constitution grants us this right; the only breach of public order in the Square was committed by the *Druzhinniki* and I cannot understand how we can be tried for it. The other aim of the demonstration was this: we demonstrate, for instance, in defense of Greek political prisoners—are we to remain indifferent to the fate of our own? As for those who organized the demonstration or took part in it—I will not name them or describe the circumstances in which it was done.

PROSECUTOR: It seems from what you say that you don't repent of anything you have done, yet seven months in solitary confinement might have made you change your attitude toward Soviet laws.

BUKOVSKY: I regard that as the most contemptible argument the Prosecution could have chosen.

PROSECUTOR: You know very little about Soviet laws. As the text of Article 125 of the Constitution says, the freedoms you mention are granted for the purpose of strengthening the Socialist system and serving the workers' interests.

BUKOVSKY: And who is to decide what is or is not in their interests? That's sheer sophistry.

PROSECUTOR: I don't understand you. You have no legal training, yet you take it on yourself to judge Soviet laws. What right have you to do this?

BUKOVSKY: If I am judged by them, I have the right to judge them.

PROSECUTOR: The Decree you denounce has been adopted by the Supreme Soviet of the USSR. How can you possibly denounce it?

BUKOVSKY: That Decree was passed virtually in secret, it has not been discussed anywhere.

JUDGE: Didn't it occur to you that you would commit a breach of the peace? What about Khaustov resisting arrest?

BUKOVSKY: I warned everybody not to create a disturbance and when I saw Khaustov resisting I called out to him to stop.

(Bukovsky asks for a number of witnesses to be called: Gruzinov, a policeman who was on duty in the Square; Colonel of the KGB Abramov; the writer Kaverin,[22] one of those who had signed the letter of protest against the Decree; and Radzievsky, who has been released. The request is refused.)

INTERROGATION OF WITNESSES

KLEYMENOV: I was patrolling the Pushkin Square district with some other members of the Squad. We were walking about in the Square near Pushkin's statue and the Rossia Cinema when at 6 P.M. a crowd of some twenty to thirty people gathered near the statue. They stood about, then they raised three banners. The slogans struck me as outrageous. I went up to a young man (it was Khaustov), introduced myself, and asked him to give me the banner. He refused. The man who held the other end dropped it; I don't know who he was.

ALSKY: How long was it after these people appeared that you went up to them?

KLEYMENOV: It's so long ago, I can't remember exactly. It must have been five to ten minutes.

ALSKY: What had they done when you went up to them?

KLEYMENOV: They had displayed the banners.

KAMINSKAYA: Would it be right to say that your intervention was provoked by the text of the slogans?

KLEYMENOV: Yes.

BUKOVSKY: What did you regard as a breach of the peace?

KLEYMENOV: The fact that there was a group of people with slogans.

KAMINSKAYA: What exactly struck you as outrageous about the texts?

KLEYMENOV: The demand for the revision of the laws— I respect Soviet laws. And there was the other slogan with the names.

KAMINSKAYA: So you knew the names?

KLEYMENOV: Yes, I work in the Town Committee of the Komsomol and by then I knew them. That was why I was outraged.

KAMINSKAYA: Do you confirm your statement during the preliminary investigation, that your intervention was provoked by the anti-Soviet nature of the slogans?

KLEYMENOV: It was provoked by the slogans but I may have described them wrongly: I would say they were outrageous rather than anti-Soviet.

BUKOVSKY: Were you wearing armbands?

KLEYMENOV: I was not.

KAMINSKAYA: Did you know in advance that there was to be a demonstration?

KLEYMENOV: No, we did not.

DVOSKIN: We had been sent to Pushkin Square because something was expected to happen that day. A group collected near the statue. I was by the newsstand with other members of the Squad. Three banners were raised near the statue; we went up to the group and asked them to give them up and disperse. I arrested a boy and girl, they came quietly with Malakhov and me. I heard some sort of a commotion going on—it turned out later that it was Khaustov being arrested—so I told Malakhov to take them to HQ and went back to help. Someone shouted "Don't resist" and Khaustov came quietly. All the others quietly dispersed, except for a few who were left standing in twos and threes. Some five to seven minutes later, a shout came from one of the groups: "Down with dictatorship! Release Dobrovolsky!" I went up to the man who had shouted and asked him what it was all about. He said that friends of his had been arrested. I asked him to come along with me to HQ and he came without resisting.

(In answer to questions by Kaminskaya, Dvoskin states that members of the Squad went up to the group only when the banners were raised, that their intervention was provoked solely by the character of the slogans, that he—Dvoskin—had not been wearing an armband and had not seen one on anyone else.)

CHERKASOV's evidence largely coincides with Dvoskin's.
GRUZINOV's evidence at Khaustov's trial is read out.

31st of August, 10 A.M.
KHAUSTOV is brought in under guard.
JUDGE: As a convicted person, you will not be required to sign an undertaking to tell the truth. We hope, never-

theless, that you will give a truthful account of the facts. Please proceed.

KHAUSTOV: I would prefer to answer questions.

JUDGE: How was the demonstration organized?

KHAUSTOV repeats the evidence he gave at his own trial and concludes: The demonstration was organized by me.

JUDGE: What part did Bukovsky play in organizing it?

KHAUSTOV: I told him my ideas and he agreed.

JUDGE: Who had the idea first, you or Bukovsky?

KHAUSTOV: I think a lot of people had it, but I personally suggested it to Bukovsky and he agreed.

JUDGE: It was organized on your initiative?

KHAUSTOV: Yes.

JUDGE: Where were the banners made? Who made them? Whom did you invite to the demonstration?

KHAUSTOV: In my opinion none of this is of the slightest interest, but the Prosecution seems very anxious to know, and I have no wish to assist the Prosecution.

JUDGE: What happened in Pushkin Square?

KHAUSTOV: We gathered at six sharp, unfurled our banners, and were attacked by *Druzhinniki*. I resisted and was taken to their HQ.

JUDGE: Why did you resist?

KHAUSTOV: These people had no armbands, they attacked us suddenly, without showing their credentials, without saying anything—I saw no reason to give up my banner.

JUDGE: Did you hear Bukovsky shout "Don't resist"?

KHAUSTOV: Yes, and then I stopped.

JUDGE: Did you know why the people, whose release you were demanding, had been arrested?

KHAUSTOV: I knew they were arrested and charged with anti-Soviet agitation and propaganda under Article 70, for producing the periodical *Phoenix*. I do not regard the periodical *Phoenix* as anti-Soviet but, even if it were, I would still consider that Article 70 is contrary to the Constitution, and so is the Decree of the 16th of September. In 1961, I was called to give evidence at the trial of Osipov and it was then I asked myself if it could be right for this article to exist in our code of criminal law. I realized that because its wording is so vague, it opens the way to every sort of persecution and witch-hunting.

PROSECUTOR: And are you at all acquainted with the principles of Soviet law?

KHAUSTOV: I am acquainted with the philosophy of law; I have read Hegel and Kant.

PROSECUTOR: And what conclusions did you draw from what you read?

KHAUSTOV: I realized that our legislation, and Article 70 in particular, is contrary to the basic universal principles of law.

PROSECUTOR: Do you think you had any moral right to denounce the Decree as unconstitutional?

KHAUSTOV: As a citizen of my country I think that I— as much as you or anyone else—have not only the right but the duty to denounce what I regard as unlawful.

MELAMED: Tell me, what books on jurisprudence have you read?

KHAUSTOV: I have already said—I read Hegel and Kant.

MELAMED: Which of their books?

79

KHAUSTOV: I won't answer that question.

MELAMED: Have you read Lenin's *The State and the Revolution?*

KHAUSTOV: Yes.

MELAMED: And what did you learn from it?

KHAUSTOV: I won't answer that question.

MELAMED: Tell me, did you consult anyone as to whether your actions would be legal?

KHAUSTOV: Yes, I asked one or two people.

ALSKY: Can you tell me whether they are people who are competent in legal matters?

KHAUSTOV: I won't answer that question.

ALSKY: Don't misunderstand me—I am not asking their names, only your opinion of their competence.

KHAUSTOV: I still refuse to answer.

MELAMED: You have a wrong conception of Soviet law. Kant and Hegel are all very well, but how are their ideas compatible with our actual conditions, with the legal basis of our State?

KHAUSTOV: I don't think they are, so long as the Soviet State exists.

(Exclamation from the public: "Typically anti-Soviet!" Khaustov is led away.)

LYUDMILA KATZ takes the stand.

JUDGE: Which of the accused do you know?

KATZ: All three. I know Kushev best.

JUDGE: Tell the Court what happened on the 22nd of January.

KATZ: I thought you were going to ask me questions. It was the Court that summoned me to give evidence.

JUDGE: How did you hear that there was to be a meeting on the 22nd of January, 1967?

KATZ: Kushev came and told me of the arrests, and that a meeting in defense of the prisoners was to be held on the 22nd.

JUDGE: Why did you go to it?

KATZ: It was in defense of my friends, I couldn't stay out of it.

JUDGE: Tell the Court what you saw.

KATZ: Banners.

JUDGE: Who was holding them?

KATZ: I didn't see.

JUDGE: Who were the boy and girl who held one of them?

KATZ: I don't know.

JUDGE: How did Bukovsky behave in the Square?

KATZ: I saw him during the scuffle with Khaustov. He was standing near him, saying, "Quiet, Viktor, don't resist." That's what he said again and again to everybody, not only to Khaustov. After that he left and I didn't see him again. All this happened before six fifteen. At six fifteen, I was very surprised to see Kushev coming along —there were very few of us left. He came up and asked me what had happened. I said banners had been displayed and Khaustov was already under arrest. Then I moved away and heard a shout: "Release Dobrovolsky."

JUDGE: You heard nothing else?

KATZ: No.

KAMINSKAYA: Did you see anyone with an armband?

KATZ: No.

BUKOVSKY: Is everybody still under arrest?

KATZ: No, Radzievsky has been released.

VOSKRESENSKY, a student from the Moscow Power Institute and a friend of Kushev's, describes him as a good, devoted comrade, a man of somewhat weak character but a gifted poet.

KUCHEROVA, after talking long and irrelevantly about her private troubles, describes how she and Bukovsky stood in a gateway, fixing the poles to a banner. She was opposed to the demonstration and tried to argue Bukovsky out of it, suggesting other forms of protest, but he said, "I have to do it."

BEZOBRAZOV, a member of the Komsomol Squad, states that there was a serious breach of the peace, he heard a lot of noise and swearing, and that he was wearing an armband.

ANATOLY LEVITIN takes the stand.

JUDGE: Which of the accused do you know?

LEVITIN: All three. Yevgeny Kushev I know well; I have met Vladimir Bukovsky several times and Vadim Delaunay once.

JUDGE: Tell us about yourself and your friendship with Kushev.

LEVITIN: I work as bookkeeper for one of the churches. Apart from that I am a religious writer—I write articles under the pen name of "Krasnov" [23] which are widely known in Church circles both here and abroad. In the summer of '65 I was having my articles typed and at the typist's I met a young man who had read some of them. We got talking about religion, philosophy, and politics. I came across him several times, then I asked him to my flat and he soon became like one of the family. Some months later, under my influence, he asked to be baptized. I am his godfather so there is a spiritual kinship between us.

JUDGE: Don't you feel responsible—morally I mean— for his being in court now?

LEVITIN: Certainly I do. All the more because he was arrested before my eyes.

JUDGE: Tell us how it happened.

LEVITIN: Late on the evening of the 21st of January, I found a handwritten note in my letter box. It invited me to a meeting of protest against the arrest of Dobrovolsky and Lashkova, to be held near the Pushkin statue at 6 P.M. on the 22nd. I went but I was late—by the time I got there it was all over. There were only a couple of small groups of young people near the statue. I saw Yevgeny Kushev standing with two other boys. I went up to him and said, "Let's go away." He said, "You go away, Anatoly Emmanuilovich." I wanted to get him away but just then Lyudmila Katz took me by the arm and drew me aside. When I looked back I saw that something had happened—Yevgeny was being led away by two men who were holding his arms. Someone said to me, "They've arrested him." I ran after him but it was too late—they pushed him into a car and drove off. And now I see him after eight months—here, pale and drawn after his long imprisonment.

JUDGE: What can you tell us about Yevgeny Kushev's views?

LEVITIN: I suppose it's his political views that interest you?

JUDGE: Not at all. What sort of a man is he?

LEVITIN: He is a man of exceptional integrity. A seeker, who needs by nature to try hard to find a meaning in life. What happened to him is the direct result of his generosity.

JUDGE: What did happen?

LEVITIN: He was driven by a generous impulse to stand up for his friends. He is very unselfish, always thinking of others, never of himself. A gifted poet, deeply interested in art, history, philosophy, he has all the makings of a brilliant writer. He believes in socialist democracy. Like all the intelligentsia, he and I believe in greater freedom of speech and of the press. But we believe in fighting for it by strictly legal means. Yevgeny and a friend of his, who has since died, Kolosov, used to edit two handwritten periodicals—*Russian Word* and *Socialism and Democracy*. They reproduced articles from Soviet periodicals, and his poems and my articles. Nothing in them was anti-Soviet. Yevgeny wanted to start a "Ryleyev" [24] club where young people could freely discuss philosophical questions and public issues. I warmly approved the idea.

PROSECUTOR: You just said that Kushev is a man of exceptional integrity. Does your idea of integrity include truthfulness?

LEVITIN: Yes, of course.

PROSECUTOR: Then how is it that you said you had influenced him and he told us that you hadn't.

LEVITIN: That's bound to be a matter of opinion. Of course he knows best whether I influenced him or not—often a teacher thinks he has just given a very good lesson, yet it turns out that the pupil has learned nothing.

PROSECUTOR: You also said he writes good poetry, yet he told us he is no good at it.

LEVITIN: You must put that down to his modesty. His poetry is very good indeed. As a poet he is attracted to heroic themes—the Decembrists, the People's Will Revolutionaries,[25] and so on.

PROSECUTOR: As his godfather, didn't it upset you that he wasn't working?

LEVITIN: That's not true. When I first met him he was working at the Lenin Library. Afterward, he went regularly to night school—except last year, when he was always being dragged off to be questioned or to mental hospitals.

ALSKY: How did you get to know Kushev?

LEVITIN: I have already told the Court. You don't seem to have been listening, Comrade.

ALSKY: What makes you think it was your influence that led him to be baptized?

LEVITIN: I was the only religious man he knew. After all, it could hardly have been the result of the investigation of his case.

ALSKY: And were you pleased?

LEVITIN: Of course I was pleased. What kind of a religious man or writer would I be if I wasn't happy when people come to believe in God? But I am most displeased to see him in court.

ALSKY: You taught him, but what did he do for you? What did you want him for?

LEVITIN: You see, I've been a teacher since I was eighteen. It's my vocation to work with young people.

JUDGE: In what year did you stop teaching in school?

LEVITIN: In 1959. I was dismissed because of my religious convictions.

ALSKY: Why did you pick on Yevgeny for the exercise of your pedagogical gifts?

LEVITIN: They are not exercised according to plan. One doesn't say: from tomorrow on, I'll exercise them. Such knowledge as I have, I am ready to impart to anyone— you, if you care to come.

ALSKY: Thank you very much! Did his mother know you had baptized her son?

LEVITIN: She probably did. But I hadn't met her until yesterday. I didn't go after Yevgeny—he came to me— and I didn't feel I had to impose myself on his family.

ALSKY: So you think you can baptize a nineteen-year-old boy without his parents' knowledge?

LEVITIN: There is a canonical rule that the Church is

not entitled to refuse baptism to anyone, and the Gospels call upon everyone without exception to be baptized.

ALSKY: Do they talk of it as flippantly as you do?

LEVITIN: That's just my manner.

KUSHEV: I want to add something. I didn't say Anatoly Emmanuilovich had no influence over me. I said he had no evil influence. And neither he nor I are Christian Democrats.

LEVITIN: If you mean in the Adenauer sense, of course not.

KAMINSKAYA: Did you see anyone wearing an armband?

LEVITIN: Yes, I did.

TATYANA LITVINOVA[26] takes the stand.

JUDGE: Which of the accused do you know?

LITVINOVA: None of them. But I was in Pushkin Square at five to six on the 22nd of January.

JUDGE: How do you remember the time so exactly?

LITVINOVA: I had just checked my watch. I stopped to look at the statue and it struck me that there were more people in front of it than usual. I wouldn't call it a crowd exactly. At that moment, some banners were raised. I don't remember if it was one after another or all three at once. Two had the same text: "Freedom for" and a list of names—three, I think, but I don't remember exactly. I think two were Dobrovolsky and Lashkova. The letters were blue on a white background. I didn't have time to read what was on the third banner. I think it began with the words "We protest." I don't remember who was holding the banners, it was dark by then, and all wore dark winter coats. Then I heard a sound of cracking wood and saw that a man, also in a dark coat, had come up and was taking the banners away. I heard somebody say not very loudly—he wasn't shouting—"Don't resist." The man whose banner had been seized was led away toward the center of the town, down Gorki Street. There were two policemen at the crossing. I asked them what was going on. They lowered their eyes and one of them said, "We haven't seen anything." Nothing more was happening in the Square. People were dispersing.

JUDGE: Who told you about today's trial?

LITVINOVA: Mrs. Bukovskaya.

JUDGE: Is she a friend of yours?

LITVINOVA: I met her here for the first time. She had rung me up and asked me to come as a witness.

JUDGE: Who told her your number?

LITVINOVA: I don't know.

JUDGE: And why did she ask you to come?

LITVINOVA: I'd like to start at the beginning. In March or April I heard about the trial of Khaustov.

JUDGE: How did you know Khaustov?

LITVINOVA: I didn't know him, I heard his name for the first time in connection with the trial.

JUDGE: Who told you about Khaustov's trial?

LITVINOVA: As we all know, court hearings in our country are public, and there was a lot of talk about this one among writers. From what I was told, I realized that

Khaustov was the man I had seen arrested, so naturally I was interested in his case. When I heard that the appeal was coming up before the Supreme Court, I went to the hearing.

JUDGE: How did you know when it would come up?

LITVINOVA: I went to Kuibishev Street and asked at the inquiry desk. At the hearing I was surprised to see that the only witnesses were those who, one way or another, had been involved in the demonstration—either taken part in it, or arrested those who had—although Pushkin Square is a busy place and other witnesses could have been found. I said so to the Prosecutor and told him that I myself could have given evidence as I was there at the time. Somebody must have told this to Bukovskaya and she found out where I live.

JUDGE: Why didn't you offer your evidence to the investigating authorities?

LITVINOVA: I didn't know that an investigation was going on, I heard only after Khaustov's trial. That was when I offered to give evidence.

JUDGE: Are you interested in legal matters?

LITVINOVA: Not exactly that. There is a special, passionately keen interest among writers in the observance of socialist legality and of the rule that trials must be public.

JUDGE: What did you think when you saw the slogans?

LITVINOVA: Nothing special. I decided that these young people must be protesting because they think some friends of theirs have been arrested unjustly. But I didn't know the names, so I couldn't speculate any further.

JUDGE: But what is your attitude to that form of protest as such?

LITVINOVA: It seems to me childish, unwise, as pointless as it is innocuous. Whom are they addressing their demands to? Nobody knows.

KAMINSKAYA: Did you notice if the movement in the Square was obstructed?

LITVINOVA: No, there was nothing like that. I forgot one detail. When the banners were raised, a woman with a child came and asked me who were the people whose names were written up. She wouldn't have come up with a small child if there had been a crowd.

ALSKY: Have you had legal training?

LITVINOVA: Unfortunately not.

ALSKY: Are there lawyers in your family? Is your father a lawyer?

LITVINOVA: No, my father was a diplomat and a professional revolutionary.

(The Prosecutor orders the question to be withdrawn.)

BUKOVSKY: Did you come across any representatives of authority in the Square?

LITVINOVA: Nobody, except those two policemen.

BUKOVSKY: Did you see anyone with an armband?

LITVINOVA: No, I did not.

ALEXANDER YESENIN-VOLPIN[27] takes the stand.

JUDGE: Where and how are you employed?

VOLPIN: I am junior research fellow at the All-Union Institute of Scientific and Technological Information.

90

JUDGE: The Court has summoned you to give evidence and I warn you of your legal obligation to give it and to speak the truth.

VOLPIN: Before I start, I must give you a message from the people outside, who can't get into the courtroom. They gave me a written statement, but some man . . .

JUDGE: I will ask you questions and you must answer them. Do you know the accused?

VOLPIN: I have known Bukovsky since the autumn of 1961. Delaunay I met about a year ago—he came to see me when I was ill. I don't know the third man in the dock. I can't tell you much about Delaunay except that he read me some poems, of which some were good, though I suppose there were bad ones too.

JUDGE: Why did he bring you his poems?

VOLPIN: I don't know. Perhaps because I once published some of my own.[28] I know Bukovsky better. We have been casually acquainted since the autumn of '61— someone had introduced us in the street. Then he came to work at the Institute. At one time I was giving lectures on philosophy for the staff and I remember him among the audience. After that we met more often, but he didn't stay long at the Institute; he went to a hospital. I didn't see him again for a long time, but meanwhile I had got to know his parents, I used to go to their house. When he came back, we met from time to time. We were on friendly terms.

JUDGE: What was the link between you and these people?

VOLPIN: I don't know that there was a link. Except of course that we are all human, which ought to be a link between you and me and you and the accused . . .

JUDGE: Does the date the 22nd of January mean anything to you?

VOLPIN: Of course. That was the day a demonstration was held in Pushkin Square to demand the revision of Article 70 and of the Decree of the 17th of September, which the demonstrators described as anti-constitutional. They also demanded the release of four prisoners.

But I really must give you that message from the people outside. They are being kept out by some men in plain clothes who call themselves *Druzhinniki* but have no armbands. One of them tore the statement from my hands while it was still being signed.

JUDGE: You ought to have followed him, then you would know what became of the statement.

VOLPIN: I am not obliged to follow a man who is not a representative of authority. The statement was a request to have the proceedings broadcast over a loudspeaker, so that they can follow—that's all they want.

JUDGE: I know, I have the statement.

VOLPIN: Then I need say no more—except that there would have been more signatures if it hadn't been snatched away from me.

Now, about the demonstration. To begin with, it was not the first of its kind dealing with legal matters. The first in recent times was on the 5th of December, 1965, when the demand was for an open trial for Sinyavsky and Daniel. I was one of those who started it. Later there

were others. In December of '65 some of the demonstrators were arrested, some of them after resisting arrest, yet all were released the same day, no one was
kept in prison—so on the 22nd of January the demonstrators might well have expected a similar outcome. It
is true that in '65 there was no Article 190/3, but that
does not account for our immunity, because if we really
had committed a serious breach of the peace, it would
still have been punishable, yet the question was not
even raised. Bukovsky and the others knew this, so they
had good reason to believe that they were legally im-
mune.

To come to the actual facts. That day I rang up
Bukovsky and asked him to meet me. I didn't know
about the demonstration but I had heard the day before
that three young men had been arrested and I wanted
to check the facts. Bukovsky said he had people at his
flat, so he could not go out but would I like to come
over, so I went. That was some time after three. I don't
remember exactly how many people there were at the
flat, nor do I remember if Delaunay was there. We all
set out together for Pushkin Square. When we got out
of the trolleybus, I counted seventeen of us, though
actually, as I knew hardly any of the demonstrators, I
might have included some who had nothing to do
with it. I had heard that many more demonstrators were
expected, so a few minutes before six I left Bukovsky's
group to see who else had arrived. At exactly six, by
the clock in the Square, I was in front of the Pushkin
statue. At that moment, before the demonstration began,

I can say for certain that I saw no demonstrators on the spot, but I did see two or three men in plain clothes, standing on the left of the statue. I went back to where I had left Bukovsky's group but they had gone—we must have missed each other in the underground passages. Then I went back to the Square—it was three minutes past six—and saw people standing quietly, holding banners. I stopped to read the slogans and was just thinking of joining the demonstration when one of the men in plain clothes went up and started taking the banners away. Only one man—Khaustov I think—resisted; the others all gave theirs up quietly. I couldn't see exactly what was happening because there was a ring of people around the place where the commotion was going on. I heard Bukovsky call out: "Quiet, don't resist!" and immediately afterward Khaustov was led away. The demonstration was virtually over, though it hadn't yet dispersed. Bukovsky was standing still. I turned to go but I didn't leave the Square at once. I walked two or three times to the entrance to the underground passage and back. Once, I looked at the clock—it was 6:17. Once, as I was coming back to the Square, I met Delaunay. I hinted that it was time to go, but he didn't listen to me; he stayed. I left. I had not seen any breach of the peace—unless you count the one committed by those men in plain clothes and without armbands, but this is not the subject of the present hearing. I only want to add one thing that occurred to me at the time, when I read the slogans . . .

JUDGE: We have heard you out. Have the Comrade

Counsels for the Defense any questions for the witness?
KAMINSKAYA: Yes, I want to know if Bukovsky regarded his demonstration as legal.
VOLPIN: Yes, of course. When the demonstrators described the Decree as anti-constitutional, I think they made a characteristic mistake: they confused the law with its interpretation.
KAMINSKAYA: Am I right in concluding from what you say that Bukovsky intended to carry the demonstration through in perfect conformity with the law and that these were his instructions to the demonstrators?
VOLPIN: Without the slightest doubt.

IRINA DELAUNAY (mother of Vadim Delaunay) takes the stand.
JUDGE: Tell the Court about yourself and your son.
IRINA DELAUNAY: I am a chemist by training. I have two children, Vadim and another boy. When they were quite small, my husband behaved very badly: he deserted me and the children. They grew up without a father. They were devoted to each other. The younger one (there are six years between him and Vadim) positively worshiped his brother. Vadim is a very good, sensitive boy. He has been writing poetry ever since he was a child. I was not too happy about it. I thought he ought to be trained for something more definite than just being a poet. But he is tremendously keen on literature.
JUDGE: Do you know his poem *Unbelief*?
IRINA DELAUNAY: He showed it to me but I wouldn't read it. In general, I avoid reading that kind of thing.

JUDGE: What kind of thing?

IRINA DELAUNAY: Well, things that haven't been officially approved.

JUDGE: Do you know Bukovsky?

IRINA DELAUNAY: Slightly.

JUDGE: Did you know about your son's other contacts, or his taking part in the meeting?

IRINA DELAUNAY: I knew nothing. It came like a bolt from the blue. I beg you to treat him leniently, to consider his youth and his good qualities.

INNA MALINOVSKAYA (mother of Kushev) takes the stand.

JUDGE: Tell the Court about yourself and your son.

MALINOVSKAYA: I am an actress by profession. I've had a very hard life. My husband and I divorced soon after Yevgeny was born, then his father died. His stepfather (I married the well-known actor Gritsenko) treated him dreadfully; he hurt and scolded and humiliated him and made ghastly scenes over every piece of food I gave the child. I divorced him; I have a six-year-old daughter, Katya, by him. Yevgeny was always very good to me, I never heard one word of reproach from him. He is my only friend, the only one who understands me.

JUDGE: Was he always quite frank with you?

MALINOVSKAYA: Yes, completely.

JUDGE: Did you know he was baptized?

MALINOVSKAYA: Yes, I knew.

JUDGE: What was your reaction?

MALINOVSKAYA: I don't look down on religion.

JUDGE and PROSECUTOR: What? Are you a believer?

MALINOVSKAYA: No, I can't call myself a believer—I was never baptized and I don't go to church. But I have my own kind of God. In general, we actors—people who depend on chance—are mostly a bit religious or superstitious: either we make the sign of the cross when we come on stage, or we spit over the left shoulder. Besides, we are always in touch with the spiritual world, with people's souls.

JUDGE: Are you or aren't you a believer?

MALINOVSKAYA: I'm a superstitious person.

JUDGE: Did you know about your son's friendship with Citizen Levitin?

MALINOVSKAYA: Yes, I knew of his friendship with Citizen—or should I say Comrade—[to Levitin] I'm so sorry, I don't know how to call you.

LEVITIN: Whatever you like.

MALINOVSKAYA: I don't know the clerical term.

LEVITIN: I am not a priest.

MALINOVSKAYA: I don't regard his influence over Yevgeny as evil. Yevgeny has been treated really savagely—they shut him up in a madhouse, they put him in with violent patients. It's true that they moved him to another ward later on. But it turns out that he was perfectly sane all the time. It was after going through all this that he was baptized, and it gave him peace of mind. I was very astonished when he told me, but I understood him very well. Yevgeny is a very gifted person. I should like to ask the Court to read his poems.

PROSECUTOR: He told us that his poems were no good.

MALINOVSKAYA: That's just his modesty, don't you believe him. He learned Spanish all on his own, and so well that his translations of García Lorca were accepted for publication by the periodical *Yunost*.

PROSECUTOR: He didn't work.

MALINOVSKAYA: He was always working! Until he was eighteen, he had no permit to work because he was at school, but even then he worked at the Lenin Library. And he went on working.

PROSECUTOR: That was not an official job.

MALINOVSKAYA: What's the difference?

ALSKY: Did you know about his going to the meeting?

MALINOVSKAYA: I knew nothing at the time. His uncle from Bulgaria was with us that day. We dined, Yevgeny had a glass of brandy, then he made a telephone call. I could hear it was a man at the other end. Yevgeny said he had to see a friend. It wasn't till the following day I heard he had been arrested. I beg you as his mother to be lenient and set him free.

INNA BUKOVSKAYA: (Vladimir Bukovsky's mother) takes the stand.

JUDGE: Tell us about your son.

BUKOVSKAYA: My son has had a very difficult life right from the start. We were always hard up at home. Vladimir is a person who easily gets carried away and, whatever he is keen on, he puts the whole of himself into it. At one time it was biology. And there were always his friends. He was always doing things for them and about them, and taking the blame for others. He went to Mayakovsky Square: they were reading poetry. Suddenly the *Druzhinniki* attacked him and beat him up. Or he photographed Djilas's book. He was so young, he was twenty-two—and they sent him to a mental hospital for a year and nine months. Perhaps he really is sick, yet now you are trying him, you treat him as sane. He is good and kind and unselfish, he has never cared about clothes and he is a devoted son to me. But he can't settle down—of the past four years he's spent nearly three locked up: the Leningrad prison mental hospital, the Serbsky Clinic, and now he's in Lefortovo. He comes out and they pick him up again. They don't give him a chance even to start to work or to study. But he's not a social parasite, and he's not a criminal. He is a grown-up man now, and I know he understands what he is doing and he would never do anything bad.

PROSECUTOR: Why is he so embittered against Soviet law?

BUKOVSKAYA: What do you mean? Vladimir is terribly keen on law.

SPEECH FOR THE PROSECUTION

We are investigating a crime which is very rare in our country. Its rarity makes it all the more dangerous. Three young men are accused of staging, in the city center, a demonstration directed against the KGB. Some of those involved and some of the witnesses fail to see that an offense has been committed under Article 190/3: they stress the fact that there was no interference with traffic, etc.

There is, indeed, no such charge in the Indictment: all it mentions is participation in—and, in the case of Bukovsky, organization of—group activities involving a grave breach of the peace. In denying this charge, the witnesses I have referred to fail to distinguish between Article 190/3 and Article 206. Both deal with serious violations of the peace, but 206 applies to a deliberate show of disrespect for society—which indeed is not mentioned in the Indictment and is not required for the application of 190/3. On the other hand, 190/3 applies only to group activities, while 206 does not.

The grounds for the application of Article 190/3 are the following: Soviet citizens have the right to express dissatisfaction with certain things including actions by the authorities, but for this there exists an established order of procedure. In staging their demonstration, the accused did not follow this procedure, thereby committing a breach of the peace. The breach of the peace was gross: gross because of its impudence—impudence is shown by the fact that they criticized existing laws and the activities of the Security Services, thereby undermining their authority. Basically, public order was violated by the slogans.

As we have seen, these activities were group activities and the part played in them by the accused was active: this is the essential point—there were others who merely attended the demonstration and they have not been charged; some of them appeared in court, but simply as witnesses.

Not so the three accused: their participation was active. Bukovsky bears the full measure of responsibility: he made up the slogans, prepared the banners, invited people to attend, and played the leading part in the demonstration. Delaunay carried a banner, refused to leave the Square, and was very active throughout. Kushev, admittedly, did not write his slogan on a banner, but I see no essential difference between writing a slogan and shouting it. Bukovsky bears the further responsibility of being the organizer.

The actions of the accused were intentional. True, the accused claim that their intention was not to create a disturbance but to heighten the citizens' sense of law. But we have seen what Bukovsky's own sense of law is like. The danger of the intention lies in its being directed at criticizing laws and discrediting the KGB.

All three accused are guilty. Many others are guilty as well: the fathers who deserted their children, the mothers and godfathers who failed to warn them against crime. Kushev's mother remained quite unruffled when her son got involved with religion. She has her own God, if you please! Naturally, the son looked for one of his own as well—and that god gave evidence in court, in the person of Kushev's godfather.

I ask the Court to find all three accused guilty. I ask the Court to sentence Vadim Delaunay to detention for one year, Yevgeny Kushev for two years, and Vladimir Bukovsky for three years, the terms to be served in camps with a normal regime.

SPEECHES FOR THE DEFENSE

MELAMED (defending Delaunay): The case is indeed, as Comrade Prosecutor has said, unusual in our country. The demonstration in question was illegal—as a lawyer I must admit this. But illegality and criminal liability are two different things, and the demonstrators are not criminally liable. Various demonstrations are organized by our public, but always on the decision of some public organization.

My client Delaunay is a gifted youth and a Soviet citizen in the full sense of the word. He has been writing poetry since childhood and has all the makings of a Soviet poet. At one time, he and a number of other young people asked permission to start a young poets' club. The authorities refused without giving a reason, and made them feel unwanted. Older people are to blame when young poets lose their way, start thinking themselves very nearly geniuses, and form mutual admiration societies. Some of you may have seen wine when it is fermenting. It foams and the foam splashes over the edge of the barrel. What does a good wine-grower do? He doesn't clap the lid on to the barrel, he carefully skims the wine, leaving it to ferment, and the wine is good as a result. But what does the bad winegrower do? He closes the barrel with the foam inside, binds it with iron hoops—and as a rule the wine turns into vinegar. That's what we do to people by our ruthlessness and severity. We turn them away, and they go to others for the care and sympathy they need—they go to the Levitins. I don't want to talk about Levitin now—he is only a witness at present—but truly, what he did to Kushev is terrible. We heard another witness, too, Volpin, a mathematician—but the fact that he is the son of a famous poet was enough to make him an attraction for the young.

Getting no support for their plan of a writers' organization, some of these young people formed the literary group SMOG. Delaunay was not a member: something about their program put him off. He is a man of his word: he takes such programs seriously, just as he does his promises. Once he has made a promise he keeps it, and this is the only reason he took part in Bukovsky's demonstration though he disagreed with its slogans. The fact that he keeps his word is to his credit even though he would have done better not to give it in this case.

I ask you not to cast him out, but to acquit him. I do not regard what he has done as an offense against Article 190/3. But even if you should disagree with me, I ask you not to impose a penalty so harsh as to destroy his bright hopes as a poet. I am sure that we will hear a lot of good of him in time.

ALSKY (defending Kushev): In four days my client will be twenty. His mother told us yesterday about his difficult childhood, and I ask you to take this into consideration. I should point out that being judged fit to

103

plead does not preclude a degree of mental instability which must be taken into account when deciding the penalty for a not too serious offense. We must remember, too, that Kushev is impressionable—as is only natural at his age when young people are like wax that can be molded to any shape. This was why he fell an easy prey to the religious fanatic Levitin.

Kushev has written a great deal, and he writes as a Soviet citizen should. Here we have before us his poem dedicated to the Paris Commune.

His encounter with Levitin was a fateful incident in his life. Militant defenders of religion are more dangerous than the unrecognized poets who were Kushev's other friends. Yesterday, Levitin asserted his right to be religious and to propagate religion; but no one has given him the right to subvert minors to religion or to use compulsion. In coming to your verdict, I ask you to keep in mind the need to protect such youngsters as Katz and Voskresensky from Levitin, for it is nothing less than inhuman to drag unstable youngsters into the Church.

As to the legal definition of Kushev's actions, my colleague has already pointed out that those of Delaunay do not constitute a criminal offense. My own task is even simpler. We know from the statements of the witnesses and of Kushev himself—which no one here has denied—that Kushev came to Pushkin Square only at 6:15, when the demonstration had already been broken up by the *Druzhinniki*. By then Khaustov was under arrest, Bukovsky had left. Kushev had not been present at the preliminary meeting at Bukovsky's flat—so insignificant was to be his role that he had simply not been asked— as a result he did not know of Bukovsky's instruction to the demonstrators not to shout. He merely went to the demonstration to which Bukovsky had invited him. He arrived late; feeling that he must at least do something, he shouted his slogan—incidentally, only two people heard him—and was immediately arrested. So that Kushev took no part in the group activity and cannot possibly be charged under Article 190/3.

I ask the Court to acquit him or, in the case of a conviction, to take into account the seven months he has already spent in prison and spare the bright new shoots which have developed in his soul during those months.

KAMINSKAYA (defending Bukovsky): My task is exceptionally complicated. I could say a great deal to show how much the difficult circumstances of my client's life mitigate his responsibility. But I am precluded from doing this. There can be no question of it because my conscience as a lawyer forces me to ask for a full acquittal on the grounds that my client has committed no offense. As I need hardly explain, I don't mean that I endorse my client's actions—I simply cannot, and indeed must not, take them seriously. But this is not the point.

The fact that it was he who organized the demonstration is admitted by Bukovsky and denied by no one. The important point is that what he did was not a crime—I mean that the essential condition on which criminal responsibility depends was lacking in his case. Demonstrations are allowed in our country—in accordance with the Constitution this freedom is guaranteed by law. It is not my view that Article 190/3 abrogates the citizens' right to hold demonstrations: criminal liability for taking part in a demonstration arises only if the demonstration is accompanied by a breach of the peace as defined by some article in our Criminal Code. The provisions of Article 190/3 cover the "organization of, or the participation in, group activities involving a breach of the peace, or clear disobedience to the legitimate demands of representatives of authority, or interference with the work of transport or other state or public institutions or services." We have heard witnesses of the most varied sort: *Druzhinniki*, demonstrators, onlookers who were there by chance, even the written statement of a member of the police force. Not one of them witnessed a breach of the peace. We know from the evidence (including that of Khaustov, who was another organizer of the demonstration) that Bukovsky gave instructions to the demonstrators, insisting on strict observance of law and order. It was not his fault that Khaustov offered resistance or that Kushev gave a shout. According to our law, the organizer is not responsible for the actions of the participants unless he has agreed to them in advance. So that even if Khaustov's and Kushev's actions are regarded as a breach of the peace, there is still no evidence of intent on Bukovsky's part.

The *Druzhinniki* did not go up to the demonstrators until the slogans had been displayed. It was the text of the slogans that drew their attention. It is the text of the slogans that the Prosecutor too regards as a breach of the peace. Yet in what conditions could their text constitute a breach of the peace? Only if the text itself were illegal, that is to say, punishable under Article 70 of the Criminal Code. However, the possibility of a charge under Article 70 has been considered and rejected by a highly competent authority. There could also be criminal liability if the slogans, without being political, offended other citizens or were against morality—then the demonstrators would be liable under other articles of the Criminal Code—but nothing of the sort is mentioned in the Indictment.

Nor does the Indictment refer to disobeying the legitimate demands of representatives of authority, or interference with transport or any other activity covered by the provisions of Article 190/3, except only an alleged breach of public order—and the Prosecutor's only argument on this point is that, in arranging their demonstration, the accused failed to comply with the established procedure for putting forward their demands. But the established procedure, of which he speaks there, is not that laid down and protected by criminal law. Offenses against public order can be of various sorts—including petty ones covered by the regulations of the City Council or other local authorities, and punishable by administrative action—usually a fine. We can't make our

own laws and find people guilty without legal grounds
—and criticism of existing laws or of the KGB is not
a crime under Article 190/3.

My client is therefore innocent and I ask for his
acquittal.

FINAL STATEMENTS BY THE ACCUSED

DELAUNAY: Before I begin, I want to assure the Court
once again that I am being completely frank. The KGB
and the Citizen Prosecutor can accuse me of anything
but deceit. My friend Vladimir Bukovsky's standards
in this respect are equally high—understandably so, for
he believes that he was perfectly right to act as he did. I
don't now feel I was right but, knowing I would appear
before a Soviet court and in so unusual a case, I believed
it my duty not to mislead the authorities in any way.
This is why I stated at my very first interrogation that
I had carried a banner at the demonstration—although,
in fact, I had not been arrested for that and Khaustov
had actually taken this whole incident upon himself.
This is also why I made other statements which could
not possibly be to my advantage. I assumed, for instance,
that the Prosecution could make use (as in fact it did) of
my arrogant reply to Colonel of the KGB Abramov
when he spoke to me in Pushkin Square; nevertheless,
I deliberately included it in my evidence.

Citizen Judges, I look to you for a fair verdict. I will
not attempt a legal definition of my actions. You, not I,

must decide whether I overstepped the boundaries of what the law allows. All I can say is that not for a moment did I imagine that, by taking part in the demonstration, I would be breaking the law. All of us who took part in it—including people who know something about legal matters, such as Yesenin-Volpin who is here in court—we were all convinced that the demonstration was not illegal. We were sure that only interference with the traffic or disobedience to representatives of authority could make it a criminal offense. This is why, when Colonel Abramov advised me to leave the Square, I asked him if I was to regard this as "an order from a representative of authority." No one had made any such suggestion to us until then. None of us resisted or disobeyed the authorities, except possibly Khaustov, and even he couldn't possibly know that the men in plain clothes who attacked him were representatives of authority. So that if I did break the law, it was neither with criminal intent nor through negligence. I knew that spontaneous demonstrations do take place. I am thinking of the one demanding an open trial for Sinyavsky and Daniel, and of the SMOG demonstration in front of the Writers' Club. Although I took no part in them, I knew that none of those who did was held criminally responsible. After the new Decree and Article 190/3 came into force, I personally took part in the silent meeting in Pushkin Square, held in protest against the attempts at a partial rehabilitation of Stalin. None of us who demonstrated in Pushkin Square on the 5th of December, Constitution

Day, was punished. I wasn't even questioned. I knew that similar meetings and demonstrations were taking place in other cities—the one in Kiev, for instance, held late last year at Babi Yar.[29] Given all this, I could not imagine that a spontaneous demonstration can, in itself, be considered illegal and treated as a serious breach of the peace. The Citizen Prosecutor himself admits that spontaneous demonstrations are allowed in our country. He gave the example of people who, rejoicing at the launching of a cosmonaut and wishing to share their joy with others, go out into the street with the homemade slogan: "Hurrah, our men are in outer space!" Well, we wanted to share our grief. Our friends had been arrested and we wanted to share our anxiety about their fate. I don't see why anyone should ask, "Whom are you addressing?" To whom is the slogan addressed: "Hurrah, our men are in outer space"? To everyone, of course. No one here in court has said that we created a disturbance in the ordinary sense of the word. So what does it mean? That the slogans were themselves a breach of public order? But they were not anti-Soviet or we would have been charged under Article 70. The only order we upset was the established order of procedure for getting in touch with the authorities about our friends—we broke it by going out into the Square with our slogan "Release Dobrovolsky, etc." I agree, the text was ill-considered to say the least, but it was the order of procedure we broke: there was no breach of the peace.

It may or may not be morally right for me to demonstrate against a law which has already been passed, but

I see nothing criminal in our demand for the revision of Articles 70 and 190. After all, it's not as if only we—Bukovsky and Delaunay—had got it into our heads to protest: the adoption of the new Decree had wide repercussions in our country. I knew, of course, the text of Article 190, or I would not have gone to the demonstration. And I knew about the letter demanding its revision and describing it as anti-constitutional. I knew the letter had been signed by such prominent people as Academician Leontovich, the writer Kaverin, the film producer Romm, and others. I had not the slightest doubt of the competence of these people, nor of their high sense of civic duty. I imagine that neither have you, Citizen Judges.

The Citizen Prosecutor asked why—if such important people as Leontovich and Kaverin had expressed their opinion in the proper way, by letter—did people like us have to go out and demonstrate, breaking the law by this very fact. Why didn't we do like them, he asks. But firstly, I don't know about the Citizen Prosecutor but I can't for my part quite visualize Academician Leontovich, who is over seventy, standing in my place with a banner in Pushkin Square. And secondly, as you, Citizen Prosecutor and Citizen Judges, must know perfectly well, a letter signed by Academicians, State Prize winners, and members of the Supreme Soviet is one thing and a letter from Bukovsky and Delaunay is another. Nobody would even read us. Demonstrating was our only possible form of protest. As a matter of fact, important people do sometimes take part in spontaneous demonstrations as well—many went to Babi Yar and, according to eyewitnesses, several famous Soviet writers took part in the silent meeting held in that same Pushkin Square on the 5th of December, 1966.

The Citizen Prosecutor holds it against me that, feeling unsure of the legality of the demonstration, I asked the advice of some older comrades instead of consulting a lawyer. But to start with, I simply had no time—I only knew about the demonstration two days in advance and I began to doubt its legality only the day before. And apart from that, I am not at all convinced that even a lawyer would have given me a foolproof answer. I say this advisedly. After our arrest we were all taken to the HQ of the *Druzhinniki,* and there I had a long talk with Colonel Abramov of the KGB, Matveyev, Secretary of the Central Committee of the Komsomol, and Mikhailov, Secretary of the Moscow Committee of the Party. Not one of them suggested that we had committed a crime and Colonel Abramov actually said this to me: "We did you a good turn, Delaunay, by arresting you when we did. Another twenty minutes and there would have been such a crowd that the traffic would have been held up, and then you, an educated young man, a poet, would have been charged with breaking the peace and sent to prison with thieves and hooligans." I ask you, Citizen Judges, if a man as competent in legal matters as Colonel of the KGB Abramov thought I could be charged under Article 190/3 only if we had blocked the traffic or disobeyed the authorities, how could I, with my less than amateurish knowledge of law, imagine that by merely taking part in a demonstration I was committing an offense? The Citizen Prosecutor stresses the fact that in spite of my doubts as to the usefulness or propriety of the demonstration, I was one of its most active participants—I brought one of the banners to the Square, I held it with Khaustov, and I stayed in the Square after the banners had been removed. Of course this was no mere accident—I had my reasons for acting as I did. I felt that, since I had, all the same, agreed to take part in a demonstration with these particular slogans, it was my duty to demonstrate and not stand aside and pretend it had nothing to do with me.

JUDGE: Accused Delaunay, have you any request to make to the Court?

DELAUNAY: No, I have no request. All I want is that the Court should not misunderstand me. If I spoke as I did now in court and before, throughout the preliminary investigation, it was not just to save my skin. I made every effort to give as objective an account of my actions as I could. This was not so simple for me, Citizen Judges. I am a writer, and I find the conditions at Lefortovo, as I did at the Serbsky Clinic, all the harder to bear. Only with difficulty have I succeeded in keeping up my will to live and to write. Of course, nothing very terrible will happen if I get three years. I don't expect I'll die or commit suicide. But whether the camps will leave me sufficient strength for creative work when I come out, of that I am not sure. One of the Public Assessors has asked:

"What can they give the world, this bunch of young poets and artists who are estranged from the people?" I would sooner not have touched on this subject, but it's not a question of me alone—this is why I found the remark particularly painful and, I venture to say, unjust. Many experts in the field of art differ from the Citizen Assessor on this point. I never asked for a pedestal or thought myself a genius, that's why I was not a member of SMOG. But after all, it's not just an obsession of mine that I've got a certain talent for poetry and that I have something to say—I've not invented it, I've been told by people who are sufficiently competent. I have not asked for them as witnesses only because my poetry is not the issue in this trial.

I admit I have made a lot of stupid mistakes recently. I think the demonstration was one of them, but this does not mean that I have nothing to say as a poet or that I am dangerous to society.

If I think the demonstration was a mistake, this is not only because the slogan "Release Galanskov, Dobrovolsky, etc." was ill-considered, but also because I never was a great believer in such gestures. I never thought they were the way to express one's point of view. It was just because I wanted to prevent such incidents that I asked our official organizations to help us start a young writers' discussion club. Given the circumstances, I felt I must take part in the demonstration, but I am more than ever convinced that I was right before.

This is all I have to say, Citizen Judges. I await a just verdict.

KUSHEV: I am sorry I shouted in the Square—I did it on the spur of the moment, without thinking. I didn't think I was doing anything illegal when I went to the demonstration, and I still don't see that we broke any law. Friendship has always been the most important thing in life for me—this is why I went. Our mothers are here—they don't think we are criminals. This has all been taken much too seriously. There's Kleymenov who says he can't even remember the details . . .

What I simply can't understand is what religion has got to do with it. Why was there such a lot of talk about it? All it did was to create a tense atmosphere—after all, religion is a purely private matter. And I can't understand why the Indictment said that, under Levitin's influence, I had become a Christian Democrat. What we both think is simply that Christianity and Socialism go together.

JUDGE: What is your request to the Court?

KUSHEV: During the investigation I have thought a lot and I have changed several of my opinions. I am grateful to the KGB Interrogator for treating me well. I ask the Court not to pass too heavy a sentence but to give me a chance to get on my feet. I ask you not to destroy my life and my work.

BUKOVSKY: I want to thank my counsel and my comrades.

When I was preparing for the trial, I expected that the Court would go fully into the motives of the accused and make a legal analysis of their actions. But it has not done anything of the sort. It went in for character defamation instead—though whether we are good or bad is completely irrelevant to the case.

I expected the Prosecutor to go in detail into the "disturbance" we are alleged to have created—who struck whom, who stepped on whose toe, and so on. But he didn't do that either.

What the Prosecutor said in his speech was, "The danger of this offense is its impudence."

JUDGE: Accused Bukovsky, why are you quoting the Prosecutor?

BUKOVSKY: I do it because I must. Please let me speak. I assure you it's not easy for me, even if I sound fluent. So, the Prosecutor regards our demonstration as impudent. Yet here I have before me the text of our Constitution: "In the interests of the workers and in order to strengthen the Socialist System, the citizens of the USSR are guaranteed by law . . . freedom to march and to demonstrate in the streets." Why was this article put in? To legalize the demonstrations of October and May Day? [30] But that wasn't necessary—everybody knows that if the Government has organized a demonstration, nobody is going to break it up. What is the use of freedom to demonstrate "for" if we can't demonstrate "against"? We know that protest demonstrations are a powerful weapon in the hands of the workers and that the right to hold them exists in every democracy. And where is this right denied? Here is *Pravda* of the 19th of August —a news item from Paris says that May Day demonstrators are being tried in Madrid. They were tried under a new law: it had recently been passed in Spain and it imposes terms of eighteen months to three years in prison for taking part in a demonstration. Note the touching unanimity of Fascist and Soviet law.

JUDGE: Accused Bukovsky, you are comparing two things which cannot possibly be compared—the actions of the Fascist Government of Spain and those of the Soviet State. That a comparison between Soviet policies and those of foreign bourgeois countries should be made in court, is an outrage. Keep to the facts of the Indictment. I object to your abusing your right to a final statement.

BUKOVSKY: And I object to your interfering with my right to defend myself.

JUDGE: You have no right to object to anything. In a trial everything depends on the decision of the judge.

BUKOVSKY: But you have no right to interrupt me. What I was saying is relevant to the facts in my case. In accordance with Article 243 of the Procedural Code, I insist that my objection be entered in the minutes.

JUDGE (to Clerk): Enter it, please.

BUKOVSKY: The Prosecutor has produced no real arguments in support of his statement. But more of this later. Not one of the witnesses has produced evidence of a serious breach of the peace having been committed in Pushkin Square—none, that is, except Bezobrazov, and perhaps his name should be allowed to speak for itself.[31]

JUDGE: Accused Bukovsky, your tone is outrageous. You have no right to insult the witness. And don't talk as if you were at a public meeting. You must address the Court.

BUKOVSKY: I'm not insulting him. Let's look at the facts.

People in plain clothes, without armbands, come along and say they are *Druzhinniki* but there is nothing to show that they are except the way they behave. *Druzhinniki* have a sensible, useful function to perform in the struggle with crime—with thieves, hooligans, and the like—and when they are on duty they always wear armbands. There's nothing in their instructions that gives them the right to break up a political meeting. Incidentally, where are their instructions? Instructions aren't laws, but if they are to have the force of law, if they can be cited in court—and this one was applied, after all, and people were arrested and brought to trial—then let them be made public and produced in the courtroom. Anyway, whatever else they say, we know that the *Druzhinniki's* instructions oblige them to wear armbands when on duty—whereas these people didn't even show us their credentials. When *Druzhinnik* Kleymenov, who has given evidence here in court, ran up to me, he shouted: "What's this filth you're putting up here? Wait till I black your eye."

There is no doubt that the whole thing was prepared beforehand, the people in the Square knew about our demonstration in advance. Look at what happened. Gruzinov, a policeman, has given evidence that he had not observed any breach of the peace and only went up to the demonstrators when a citizen in plain clothes ordered him to arrest one of us. Was this man a *Druzhinnik?* No. Would an experienced policeman have failed to recognize him as a *Druzhinnik* if the man had had an armband? Of course not. Who was he, then? Why should Gruzinov comply with the request of one private citizen to arrest another who had not broken the peace? Obviously he had had his instructions, and they had been sufficiently specific.

We can be sure that Colonel of the KGB Abramov wasn't there as a private citizen. It's most improbable that he was merely out for a stroll, nor do his actions suggest that he was. It's unfortunate that the Court has not subpoenaed him—his evidence could have been at least as important as that of many of the other witnesses.

Please note that I haven't so far used the word "provocation," but this is what it looks like. What else, indeed, can we call it? Imagine yourself on May Day, walking along with a banner, and a citizen in plain clothes, without an armband, grabbing it and taking it away from you—what happens in such a case? Obviously, if you'll forgive the expression, he gets it in the neck! And isn't that what the *Druzhinniki* were counting on? Isn't that why Colonel Abramov had turned up in the Square?—to be there at the right moment and to seize on a pretext for a criminal charge? What he said to Delaunay at the HQ of the *Druzhinniki* is interesting from this point of view: "If we hadn't stopped the demonstration in time, you, Delaunay—an intellectual, a poet—would have found yourself in prison with thieves and hooligans."

And why were so many houses searched? Why search the house of a man who has broken the peace? To remove the objects he used in creating the disturbance? But there was nothing to remove from our houses—we had

119

brought everything with us to the Square. What was there to look for? Cobblestones we meant to throw? At a pinch it would be understandable if only our own houses had been searched—but why those of the witnesses and of complete outsiders [lists names]? Why all this? I understand, of course, that house searches are a means of tracing and identifying other people involved in the case. But it is unthinkable that so many searches were necessary just because of a disturbance in a square. Why were we shown photos and asked to identify people who had nothing to do with the demonstration? All this is understandable only if the searches were conducted by the KGB.

The Security Services in our country play the role of the police. How can there be any talk of democracy when we are watched and followed at every step? Their job is to catch spies! Why are we questioned about our friends, or about what we were doing two or three years ago and so on and so forth? I recognize the important role of the KGB in the defense of security. But what is their business in this case? There are no external enemies involved. Were they looking for internal ones? There were no grounds for the Security Services to interfere. But let's take a look at how our case was handled.

Why did it drag on for seven months? And why, incidentally, were we put at once into the investigation prison of the KGB? I won't take up the time of the Court with a description of the conditions, but they are, after all, different. In an ordinary prison the prisoners are seven or eight to a cell, here they are two or three.

Several months of it are bound to tell on a prisoner's mental state. The rules about food and parcels are quite different as well. Why was the investigation dragged out for seven months? I can think of only one explanation: for those in charge to find some way of covering up their tracks in this ugly business. And when it was impossible to drag it out any longer, the procedings were made so secret that no one could get in and convince himself of their illegality.

The investigation was started by the Prosecutor's Office, yet the warrant for my arrest was signed by Captain Smelov of the KGB. At the end of three months the Prosecutor's Office handed the case over to the KGB. This was against the Code of Procedure: Article 125 of that Code strictly defines the sphere of competence of the KGB and this does not include cases tried under Article 190 of the Criminal Code. More than this—on the very day when the Decree introducing Article 190 was adopted, another Decree was passed, which supplemented Article 125 of the Procedural Code with the instruction that cases falling under Article 190 have to be handled by the Prosecutor's Office. Now, had there been grounds for charging us under Article 70 of the Criminal Code, then the KGB would have been justified in taking over—but what should it have done first? It should have charged us under this Article. This it did not do. Was there no investigation under Article 70? Yes, there was. This is shown by some of the questions put to the witnesses, and anyway, there is a document in the file that proves it: there is an order terminating the investigation under Article 70, and you can't terminate what was never begun. [Lists other breaches of the Procedural Code.]

JUDGE: Accused Bukovsky, none of this is of any interest to us. You must keep closer to the Indictment. How, do you think, is any of this relevant to the outcome of your trial?

BUKOVSKY: I have already said that you have no right to interrupt me. The relevance of what I say is this: what do you think it was like for me in prison, being accused of an offense against Article 70 and the investigation proceeding along those lines, without my having been charged with it? It's all these lawless actions of the KGB that the Prosecution is covering up by trying, without proof, to support charges under Article 190 of the Criminal Code. Illegalities have been committed in the course of the investigation—it's my duty to speak out about them and this is why I am speaking out.

We demonstrated in defense of legality. I cannot understand why the Office of the Prosecutor, one of whose duties is to safeguard the rights of the citizens, sanctions such actions by the *Druzhinniki* and the KGB.

I must now explain our slogans. We demanded the release of Galanskov, Dobrovolsky, Lashkova, and Radzievsky. None of them has been convicted so far, and Radzievsky, for one, has been released. What if they should all be cleared in the end? What would then be criminal in our demand?

As for our other slogan—we were not protesting against laws as such. We demanded the revision of

Article 70 and of the Decree of the 16th of September. Was this really an illegal action on our part? We protested against an anti-constitutional decree. Was this an anti-Soviet demand? We are not alone in thinking it anti-constitutional. A group of intellectuals, including Academician Leontovich, the writer Kaverin, and others, addressed the same demand to the Presidium of the Supreme Soviet of the USSR.

Isn't the Constitution the basic law in our country? I shall read the full text of Article 125: "In the interests of the workers and in order to strengthen the Socialist system, the citizens of the USSR are guaranteed by law:

(a) freedom of speech
(b) freedom of the press
(c) freedom of meeting and assembly
(d) freedom of marching and demonstrating in the streets.

To secure these rights the authorities will provide the workers and their organizations with the use of printing presses, paper, public premises, streets—yes, Citizen Prosecutor, streets!—transport and anything else they may need for the exercise of these rights."

Now about Article 70. We asked for its revision because it was too loosely worded. Here is the text: "Agitation or propaganda carried out with the purpose of weakening or subverting the Soviet regime or of committing particularly dangerous crimes against the State, the dissemination for the said purposes of slanderous inventions discrediting the Soviet political and social system, as also the dissemination or production or harboring for the said purposes of literature of a similar content, is punishable by six months to seven years of detention with or without a further period of two to five years of exile."

The Article covers offenses as widely different as agitation and propaganda with a view to committing exceptionally serious crimes against the State on the one hand, and, on the other, slanderous statements about the social order. The range of penalties is also much too wide—from half a year to seven years. The legal commentary on this Article breaks it up into fourteen points. The text ought surely to be revised along these lines and the penalties be made more specific. This would reduce the chances of arbitrary interpretation. It is true that Article 190/1 is a step in the right direction but not enough to bring it fully in line with the Constitution.

JUDGE: Accused Bukovsky, we happen to be lawyers, and presumably, everybody in this courtroom has been through high school. We quite realize that you have only just come across these legal problems and that you find them interesting. We understand and applaud your interest, but you don't have to talk about it at such length. What you must understand is that we have to find you guilty or innocent, we have to decide your fate. Perhaps later on you'll join the Legal Faculty of Moscow University and there, during the seminars, you will discuss these questions on a more sophisticated level.

BUKOVSKY: No, I will not join it. And I object to the Prosecutor accusing us of being ignorant and frivolous in legal matters. I do know the laws, and I talk about them seriously. If, however, what I have been saying is so well known, then I am still more at a loss to understand how the Prosecutor can think that to criticize the laws is a crime.

Article 125 says in its preamble that "in the interests of the workers and to strengthen the Socialist System," certain liberties are guaranteed by law to the citizens of the USSR. It's perfectly clear that neither legally nor grammatically can this be made to mean that the freedoms which the Article lists—and which include freedom of meeting and demonstration—are granted on condition that they are exercised only with the express purpose mentioned in the preamble. We know that freedom of speech and of the press is, in the first place, freedom to criticize. No one has ever been forbidden to praise the Government. If these articles about freedom of speech and of the press have been put into the Constitution, then the Government must have the patience to listen to criticism. Which are the countries that forbid their citizens to criticize the Government and to protest against its actions? Are they the capitalist countries? No, we know that in the bourgeois countries there exist Communist Parties which make it their deliberate purpose to undermine the regime. In the USA the Communist Party was banned—but the Supreme Court pronounced that the ban was unconstitutional and restored the Party to all its rights.

JUDGE: Accused Bukovsky, this has nothing to do with the charges against you. You must see that this Court is not competent to decide the issues you raise. Our duty is not to judge the laws but to apply them.

BUKOVSKY: Again you interrupt me. Can't you see how difficult it is for me to speak?

JUDGE: The Court will go into recess for five minutes.

BUKOVSKY: That's not what I asked for, I've nearly finished; you are breaking the continuity of my final statement.

(Judge declares five minutes' recess.)

After the recess:

JUDGE: Accused Bukovsky, you may proceed with your final statement, but I warn you that if you go on criticizing the laws and the activities of the KGB, I shall have to interrupt you.

BUKOVSKY: Don't you see, our case is very complicated. We are accused of criticizing the laws. I therefore have the right to raise these basic legal issues in my final statement and I have to do it.

But there are other issues as well—integrity and civic courage. You are judges, you are assumed to have these qualities. If you really have integrity and civic courage, you will reach the only possible verdict in this case—"not guilty." I realize that this is very difficult . . .

PROSECUTOR (interrupting): I draw the attention of the Court to the fact that the defendant is abusing his right to a final statement. He criticizes the laws, he discredits the activities of the KGB, now he starts insulting us—a new offense is being committed. As Prosecutor I must stop this and I call upon you to require the accused to speak only of the substance of the charges against him— otherwise we can go on forever listening to every sort of criticism of the laws and the Government.

JUDGE: Accused Bukovsky, you have heard what the Prosecutor said. I permit you to speak only of the substance of the charge.

BUKOVSKY (to Prosecutor): You accuse us of trying to discredit the KGB by our slogans, but the KGB has discredited itself so effectively that there is nothing we can add. [To Court]: It is the charge I am talking about. But what the Prosecutor wants me to say, he won't hear from me. For there is no substance in the charge against us, we have not committed any crime. I absolutely don't repent of having organized the demonstration. I believe it has done its job and, when I am free again, I shall organize other demonstrations—always, of course, like this one, in perfect conformity with the law. I have nothing more to say.

VERDICT AND SENTENCE

(For full text, see Appendix III.)

The Court found the defendants guilty, Bukovsky as organizer of the demonstration and all three as its active participants. Bukovsky was sentenced to three years in a corrective labor camp with a normal regime, the term to run from the date of his arrest, the 26th of January, 1967. Kushev and Delaunay received suspended sentences of one year each in similar camps.

Bukovsky's counsel appealed to the Supreme Court, which heard the case on the 16th of October, 1967, and left the sentence unchanged. (For full text of its findings, see Appendix IV.)

CONDUCT OF THE TRIAL

The atmosphere outside the courtroom and the building was much the same as during Khaustov's trial. The main difference was that, as this time the news had leaked out a little earlier, at least forty people turned up. Many arrived half an hour or even an hour before the hearing. Evidently in view of this, the authorities in charge took even stricter measures to prevent them from attending this "public" trial. The corridor leading to the courtroom was blocked. At first there was only one policeman on duty, explaining to the crowd that the relatives of the accused would be admitted first: "Then if there's any room left, we'll let you in as well." The Court Commandant admitted four relatives but everyone else was kept out. Soon after ten, a large group of young men swept past the policeman who, this time without asking any questions, flung the door wide open for them; many of those present recognized them as members of the Komsomol Operational Squad. A young man, who had been waiting and tried to slip in with them, was at once seized by the arms and thrown out. Some of this group remained on guard outside the courtroom door, others mingled with the public and this not only in the building but in the street outside where, together with some older men, they stood or strolled among the real members of the public, trying to overhear what was being said, peering over the shoulders of those who were taking notes, and, above all, doing everything in their power to protect Soviet citizens from contact with the foreign press correspondents who gathered round the building in ever-increasing numbers. Two people who dared to talk to these journalists were arrested and taken to the police station where their identity papers were checked. One of them is reported to have been jailed for a week, allegedly for "petty hooliganism." In one case the film was removed from a reporter's camera and exposed to the light: he had used it to take photographs of the building and of the crowd gathered in front of it. Another incident was described during the trial by one of the witnesses, Volpin.

The part played by the Security Services in the arrangements for the trial is proved if only by the following incident. A woman who was one of the crowd outside the courtroom door was a few days later arrested and taken for a "talk" with the KGB at their offices in Dzerzhinsky Street. During the talk, she was repeatedly asked, "Who told you there was to be a trial?" and "Who else was outside the courtroom?"—questions which were completely illegal and which she refused to answer. While she was waiting to be interviewed, she saw, walking down the corridor of this building where only employees of the KGB were allowed to come and go unaccompanied, the man who a few days earlier had been giving orders in the role of "Commandant" at the Moscow City Court.

As to the way the trial was conducted, the record speaks for itself. We need stress only one circumstance. In each case, great significance was attached to the political, philosophical, legal, and even religious views of the defendants. (Note the interrogation of Khaustov at both his own and Bukovsky's trial, questions put to Kushev, to Bukovsky, passages in the so-called "descriptive" part of the Indictment, such as "Bukovsky, an opponent of Communist ideology," "Kushev, influenced by the religious fanatic Levitin [Krasnov] and imbued with Christian Democratic ideology," etc.) The Indictment also brings in encounters with a certain "emissary of the NTS," even though, according to the same Indictment, "no subversive action followed." If there was nothing criminal about them, why are they there? And what in any case have they to do with the alleged breach of the peace? In the course of the trial itself, they were not even mentioned . . . The interrogation of Khaustov, of his mother, of Levitin, the speeches of Alsky and Melamed with their references to religious matters, all leave a discouraging and puzzling impression. Was Kushev tried for being baptized and believing in God? No. There is not a word about this in the verdict.

Article 18 of the Universal Declaration of Human Rights proclaims: "Everyone has the right to freedom of thought, conscience, and religion; this right includes freedom to change his religion or his belief, and freedom, either alone or in community with others and in public or private, to manifest his religion or belief in teaching, practice, worship, and observance." Article 124 of the Constitution of the USSR also guarantees freedom of conscience.

AFTER THE TRIAL

The only time the case of the demonstrators was mentioned in the Soviet press was in the following news item in *Evening Moscow* on the 4th of September, 1967:

AT THE MOSCOW CITY COURT

From the 30th of August to the 1st of September, the Moscow City Court heard the cases of V. K. Bukovsky, V. N. Delaunay, and Ye. I. Kushev, persons of no definite occupation, accused of a breach of the peace in Moscow.

Charged under Article 190/3 of the Criminal Code of the RSFSR, all three defendants pleaded guilty and told the court about their criminal actions. Their guilt was confirmed by the evidence of many witnesses.

Bukovsky had not been working for a long time and had repeatedly been warned by the authorities for his anti-social acts of hooliganism. It was also his fault that Delaunay and Kushev were with him in the dock.

The court sentenced Bukovsky to three years' detention and passed suspended sentences of one year each on Kushev and Delaunay.

Volpin sent the following letter to the Editor:

To The Editor of *Evening Moscow*

From Citizen Alexander S. Yesenin-Volpin,
17 Festivalnaya Street, Flat 1,
Moscow, A–445.

An item in your issue of the 4th of September, 1967 (No. 207, bottom of third page), headed "At the Moscow City Court," wrongly states that all three defendants pleaded guilty. The verdict, published on the 1st of September, states that Bukovsky pleaded not guilty. This mistake (if it can be so-called) needs to be corrected in your newspaper.

Should the correction be published in *Evening Moscow,* please let me know, if possible in advance.

From the final statements of Kushev and Delaunay, it was clear that the sense in which they regarded themselves as guilty was not the legal one and that they left the legal definition of their actions to the Court.

I think your readers have the right to expect greater accuracy from you in such matters, and this mistake (which may be unintentional on the part of your paper) should be corrected as well.

Many of your readers have also heard the case wrongly reported by the "Voice of America." This radio station is often accused by the Soviet press of lying, but this does not give it any right to compete with other liars.

5th of September, 1967   VOLPIN

A similar protest was addressed to the Editor by the writer Natalia Ilyina. At the end of her letter she pointed out that such distortions of fact contribute to the rise of cynicism and lack of faith among young people.

The case went on being discussed both inside the country and abroad. Among others, *The Morning Star,* organ of the British Communist Party, commented on it regretfully.

The possibility of a truthful account reaching the public worried the KGB.

On the 3rd of October, 1967, P. M. Litvinov addressed the following letter to the Editors of *Izvestia, Literary Gazette, Komsomolskaya Pravda, Moscow Komsomol, Morning Star, Humanité,* and *Unita*:

I regard it as my duty to bring the following to the attention of the public.

On the 26th of September, 1967, I was summoned by the KGB (Committee of State Security) to appear before Gostev, a KGB official, at 2 Dzerzhinsky Square, Room 537. Another KGB official, who did not give his name, was present during our conversation.

After it was over, I wrote the conversation down immediately and as fully as I could remember, because it clearly revealed tendencies which should be made public and which cannot fail to alarm progressive people in the Soviet Union and in the world outside. The text of the conversation follows. I vouch for the accuracy of the substance of what was said between the KGB official and myself.

GOSTEV: Pavel Mikhailovich, we have received information that you, with a group of other people, intend to reproduce and distribute the minutes of the recent trial of Bukovsky and others. We warn you that, if you do this, you will be held criminally responsible.

I: Irrespective of whether I intend to do this or not, I cannot see how such an action could be punishable as a crime.

GOSTEV: That will be decided by the Court that tries you. All we want to do is warn you that, should such a record be distributed in Moscow or in other cities, or appear abroad, you will be held responsible.

I: I have a good knowledge of our laws and cannot imagine which of them would be broken by the compilation of such a document.

GOSTEV: There is such a law—Article 190/1. Look in the Criminal Code and you'll see it.

I: I know that article very well (incidentally, cases investigated under it are not within the competence of the KGB); I could recite it to you by heart. It deals with slanderous statements discrediting the Soviet State and social order. How can it be slander to publish the record of a case heard before a Soviet court?

GOSTEV: Well, your record will be a biased distortion of the facts and a slander on the actions of the Court.*

* The commentary to the Criminal Code of the RSFSR defines slander as deliberately lying statements, i.e., criminal responsibility arises only if the facts are distorted with malicious intent.

This will be proved by the agency competent to handle such cases.

I: How can you know that in advance? Anyway, instead of carrying on this absurd conversation and starting a new case, you should yourselves publish the minutes of the trial and kill the rumors circulating in Moscow. I met an acquaintance yesterday and she talked to me such nonsense about the case, it made me sick to hear it.

GOSTEV: Why should we publish it? It was an ordinary case of breach of the peace.

I: If it was, that makes it even more worthwhile giving out the facts—so that everyone can see that it really was ordinary.

GOSTEV: All the information about it was published in *Evening Moscow* on the 4th of September. That gives all the information anybody needs to have.

I: To begin with, there's very little—if the reader hasn't heard about the case already he won't understand what the paper is talking about. And secondly, the information is false and slanderous. It's the Editor of *Evening Moscow,* or whoever gave him the information, who ought to be sued for slander . . .

GOSTEV: Pavel Mikhailovich, that information is perfectly accurate. Remember that.

I: It says that Bukovsky pleaded guilty. But I was interested in the case and I know for certain that he did *not* plead guilty.

GOSTEV: What difference does it make what he pleaded? The Court found him guilty, that means he is guilty.

I: I wasn't talking about the verdict—and neither was

the newspaper—I was talking about whether the defendant himself had admitted his guilt, which is a completely independent legal concept. And then the paper says that Bukovsky had committed "anti-social acts of hooliganism" in the past. Whatever else you say about his actions, they can't possibly be called "acts of hooliganism."

GOSTEV: Breach of public order is hooliganism.

I: But is any breach of regulations hooliganism? If I cross the road in the wrong place, does that make me a hooligan?

GOSTEV: Pavel Mikhailovich, you are not a child. You know perfectly well what we are talking about.

I: And anyway, more ought to be told about Bukovsky —for instance, how the *Druzhinniki* arrested him during a poetry reading in Mayakovsky Square, and took him to a police station and beat him up.

GOSTEV: That's not true, it's impossible!

I: His mother says that's what happened.

GOSTEV: His mother might have told you anything . . .

I: It wasn't me she told—I don't know her—she told the Court and no one interrupted her or accused her of slander.

GOSTEV: She'd have done better to tell you about how she was summoned and warned about her son's behavior. We can summon your parents, too. Anyway, keep this in mind, Pavel Mikhailovich: the account in *Evening Moscow* is perfectly truthful and gives all the information that Soviet citizens are supposed to have about this case, and we warn you that even if this record is not compiled by you or any of your friends, but by anyone at all, you are the one who will be held responsible.

I: That's interesting. You are talking about legal responsibility, yet according to the law, the responsibility for an action rests on the one who has committed it.

GOSTEV: You can prevent this happening to you.

I: But you still have not explained to me how such an action could be dangerous or punishable.

GOSTEV: You understand perfectly well that such a record could be used against us by our ideological enemies, especially on the eve of the 50th anniversary of the Soviet regime.

I: But I don't know of any law that makes it punishable to circulate a non-secret document, simply on the grounds that it could be used for this or that purpose. A lot of critical articles from the Soviet press could also be misused by someone.

GOSTEV: You must know perfectly well what we are talking about. We are only warning you, but the court will prove you guilty.

I: I have no doubt it will—that's clear, if only from the trial of Bukovsky. Besides, my friend Alexander Ginzburg is in prison for just the kind of thing you are warning me against.

GOSTEV: When Ginzburg is brought to trial, you'll know what he did. If he is innocent he will be acquitted. Do you really think that today, when the Soviet regime is in its 50th year, a Soviet court would bring in a wrong verdict?

I: Then why was Bukovsky tried in secret?

GOSTEV: His trial was public.

I: But no one could get in.

GOSTEV: Those whose business it was, got in. The public was represented and all the seats were filled. We weren't going to hire a hall for this case.

I: In other words, the trial was not public in fact.

GOSTEV: We don't propose to argue with you, Pavel Mikhailovich, we are simply *warning* you. Imagine if all the world were to hear that the grandson of the great diplomat Litvinov was involved in such a thing—it would be a blot on his memory.

I: Well, I don't think he would blame me. Can I go?

GOSTEV: Certainly. The best thing you can do now is go home and destroy what you've got there.

I know that a similar conversation with Alexander Ginzburg took place two months before his arrest.

Such actions by the Security Services are tantamount to open blackmail and I protest against them.

I ask you to publish my letter so that, in case of my arrest, the circumstances leading up to it should be publicly known.

> P. M. LITVINOV,
> Assistant Professor of Physics at the
> Moscow Institute of Sensitive Technology
> 8 Alexei Tolstoy Street, Flat 78,
> Moscow K – 1

3rd of October,
1967

The letter was neither published nor even so much as acknowledged by any of the seven editors to whom it was sent.

The letter from the former Major General of the Soviet Army, P. G. Grigorenko, gives a full account of the moral and legal aspects of the case.[32]

APPENDICES

APPENDIX I

VERDICT OF THE MOSCOW CITY COURT

on the 16th of February, 1967

The Judicial Collegium of the Moscow City Criminal Court, consisting of Chairman Panteleyeva and People's Assessors Mikhin and Biryukov, having—with the assistance of Clerk of the Court Fomicheva and the participation of Prosecutor Starosvetov and Defense Counsel Kallistratova—heard in open court the case of:

Khaustov, Viktor Alexandrovich (born on the 25th of June, 1938, in the City of Moscow, Russian, non-Party, secondary education, unmarried, no previous criminal record, working as a paperhanger at a furniture-repair factory in the Pervomaysky district of the City of Moscow, residing at 25 Elektrozavodskaya Street, Flat 5, Moscow)—

charged under Articles 190/3 and 206/2 of the Criminal Code of the RSFSR—

finds that:

Khaustov, V. A., being acquainted with Dobrovolsky, A. A., Galanskov, Yu. T., and other persons who had been arrested and charged under Article 70 of the Criminal Code of the RSFSR, and adopting an illegal method of demanding their release and protesting against Articles 70 and 191/1–3 of the Criminal Code of the RSFSR, acted as one of the organizers of group activities involving a grave breach of the peace in Pushkin Square on the 22nd of January, 1967, and took an active part therein together with Kushev, Delaunay, Bukovsky, Gabay, and others.

Khaustov's organizing role consisted in his arranging the place and time of the meeting, notifying a number of people, inviting them to attend, and, upon their arrival in the Square, jointly with them displaying three banners with the slogans, "We demand the revision of the anti-constitutional Decree and of Article 70" and "Release Dobrovolsky, Galanskov, Lashkova, and Radzievsky," having previously himself taken part in manufacturing these banners.

When the group was requested, by members of the Komsomol Operational Squad, *Druzhinniki* Bezobrazov, Vesna, and others, to relinquish their banners and disperse, Khaustov refused to comply and committed acts of hooliganism, using obscene language, resisting arrest by the *Druzhinniki*, and, in so doing, striking with a pole Kleymenov on the shoulder and Vesna on the leg. For these offenses Khaustov was taken to the HQ of the *Druzhinniki*.

On being interrogated, Khaustov pleaded guilty to part of the charge. He admitted that he had played an active part in convening and organizing a gathering of citizens who shared his views, but denied that he had thereby committed a breach of the peace. He admitted that he had resisted persons who later turned out to be

Druzhinniki but denied that he had committed acts of hooliganism.

The charges against Khaustov are supported by the following evidence:

As stated by witnesses Kleymenov, Vesna, Bezobrazov, Dvoskin, and others, on the 22nd of January, 1967, they, being *Druzhinniki,* were patrolling the district of Pushkin Square. At about 6.00 P.M. some thirty young people gathered in the Square, unfurled banners inscribed with slogans demanding the release of certain prisoners and the abolition of Articles 70 and 190 of the Criminal Code, and, upon being requested to relinquish the banners, refused to comply.

As stated by himself, Kleymenov requested that Khaustov relinquish his banner, but the latter continued to stand holding it and, when Kleymenov tore the slogan down, held on to the pole, resisted Kleymenov, tried to knock him down, and struck him on the back.

Vesna, in his evidence, confirmed that Khaustov had resisted arrest and, in so doing, struck Kleymenov and used an obscene expression.

The fact of Khaustov's resistance and use of obscene language was also confirmed by witness Bezobrazov.

All the above activities, of which Khaustov was an organizer, constitute a grave breach of the peace.

Witness Bezobrazov also stated that a number of citizens, who were near the Square, were outraged by the behavior of Khaustov's group. After Khaustov had been arrested and removed to the HQ of the *Druzhin-*

niki, the young people who remained in the Square continued to shout various slogans. Other members of Khaustov's group who have been arrested are Delaunay, Gabay, and Kushev.

In explaining his actions, Khaustov stated that he disagreed with certain laws which had recently been passed, and that this was one of his motives in behaving as he did.

Khaustov's actions are covered by the provisions of Articles 190/3 and 206/2 of the Criminal Code of the RSFSR.

Khaustov's refusal to comply with the legitimate demands of the *Druzhinniki,* his ensuing resistance, use of obscene language in a public place, and his striking Kleymenov with a stick, constitute malicious hooliganism.

In arriving at its verdict, the Judicial Collegium takes into account the socially dangerous character of his offense on the one hand and also the fact that he has no previous criminal record on the other.

In accordance with Articles 303 and 315 of the Procedural Code of Criminal Law of the RSFSR, the Judicial Collegium sentences:

Khaustov, Viktor Alexandrovich, found guilty under Articles 190/3 and 206/2 of the Criminal Code of the RSFSR, to detention for a term of three years under Article 190/3 and of two years under Article 206/2, the two terms to run concurrently as from the 22nd of January, 1967, and to be served in a corrective labor colony with a severe regime.

Khaustov is to remain under guard.

The three banners confiscated from Khaustov and others are to be destroyed.

An appeal against the sentence to the Supreme Court of the RSFSR may be lodged within seven days.

Signatures

PANTELEYEVA (Chairman)

MIKHIN and BIRYUKOV (People's Assessors)

Counsel for the Defense S. B. Kallistratova lodged an appeal with the Supreme Court of the RSFSR, which heard the case on the 31st of March.

APPENDIX II

VERDICT OF THE SUPREME COURT OF THE RSFSR

31st of March, 1967

The Judicial Collegium of the Supreme Court of the RSFSR, consisting of Chairman N. S. Romanov and members of the Court A. V. Kiselyova and A. V. Yevdokimenko, having, on the 31st of March, 1967, heard the appeal of Defendant Khaustov and his Defense Counsel Kallistratova against the sentence passed on him by the Moscow City Court on the 16th of February, 1967, whereby—

Khaustov, Viktor Alexandrovich, born in 1938 in

Moscow, Russian, non-Party, secondary education, unmarried, working as a paperhanger at a furniture-repair factory in the Pervomaysky district of Moscow, no previous criminal record, was sentenced to detention for a term of three years under Article 190/3 and to two years under Article 206/2 of the C.C. of the RSFSR, the terms (in accordance with Article 40 of the C.C. of the RSFSR) to be served concurrently in a corrective labor camp with a severe regime;

having heard the opinion of Judge Yevdokimenko, the explanations of Defense Counsel Kallistratova, and the conclusions of Prosecutor A. V. Koshkaryova, who submitted that the sentence should be left unchanged, the Judicial Collegium has established that:

Khaustov is guilty of being one of the organizers of group activities involving a grave breach of the peace in Pushkin Square in the City of Moscow and, in the course of these activities, committing acts of malicious hooliganism.

The offense was committed on the 22nd of January, 1967, in the following circumstances (description as on page 144).

At his trial, Khaustov pleaded guilty to part of the charges, i.e., to having organized a gathering of persons who shared his views, in the course of which banners were unfurled in the Square, and to having resisted arrest. He denied having committed acts of hooliganism.

In their appeal against the verdict the defendant and his counsel claim that Khaustov's actions were an offense

148

under Article 191 of the C.C. of the RSFSR only, inasmuch as Khaustov had resisted representatives of the public (not of the authorities), and this had been his only offense.

Defense Counsel also appealed for a sentence not involving detention on the grounds that Khaustov had been engaged in socially useful work, held good references from his employers, and nothing reprehensible had been noted in his previous conduct.

Having examined the evidence in the case and discussed the arguments for the appeal, the Judicial Collegium finds that the verdict was justified by the evidence before the Court.

Khaustov admitted that he had organized the gathering in the Square for the purpose of publicly voicing the demands of the group which he had organized, and that slogans were displayed demanding the revision of an article of the Criminal Code and the release of persons known to him, convicted under Article 70 of the Criminal Code of the RSFSR,* that he had taken part in manufacturing these banners and that he had resisted arrest.

His guilt is also confirmed by the evidence of witnesses Kleymenov, Vesna, Bezobrazov, Dvoskin, Malakhov, and others, who had been eyewitnesses of the offense and, as *Druzhinniki,* taken part in restoring order in the Square and in arresting Khaustov.

The evidence shows that when Kleymenov asked

---

* Ginzburg, Galanskov, and Lashkova were not in fact tried until January, 1968.

Khaustov to relinquish his banner, Khaustov continued to hold it, resisted arrest, tried to knock Kleymenov down, and used a pole to beat him on the back and Vesna on the leg.

The evidence of witness Bezobrazov confirms that citizens who were in the vicinity of the Square were outraged by the behavior of Khaustov's group, and that, after the latter's arrest, members of his group who remained in the Square continued to shout slogans. Delaunay, Gabay, Kushev, and other members of the group were arrested.

In the circumstances the Moscow City Court rightly reached the conclusion that the activities of the group, organized by Khaustov and others, involved a grave breach of the peace in a public square of the City of Moscow, and that these activities are an offense under Article 190/3 of the Criminal Code of the RSFSR.

The arguments in support of the appeal, to the effect that neither Khaustov nor the other members of the group had intended to commit a breach of the peace, are unconvincing and refuted by the evidence in the case and by Khaustov's actions in Pushkin Square.

As to the sentence passed on Khaustov under Article 206/2 of the C.C. of the RSFSR, the Collegium finds it necessary to change this as the evidence proves that, in striking *Druzhinnik* Kleymenov, Khaustov was not motivated by hooliganism but was merely resisting arrest, at which time he also used obscene language.

The above offense is covered by the provisions of Article 191 (not 206) of the C.C. of the RSFSR.

In deciding the penalty the Moscow City Court took into account the socially dangerous nature of the offense and the evidence regarding Khaustov's character; the Collegium can therefore see no grounds for mitigating the sentence and considers that, in view of the violence displayed by Khaustov in the course of resisting arrest, he was properly sentenced to detention.

Given the above facts, and in accordance with Articles 332 and 339 of the Procedural Code of Criminal Law of the RSFSR, the Judicial Collegium

decides:

to change the verdict passed on V. A. Khaustov by the Moscow City Court on 16th February, 1967, re-qualifying his offense as one against Article 191/1 of the C.C. of the RSFSR (not Article 206/2), and sentencing him under this Article to detention for two years, the term to run concurrently with that of three years under Article 190/3, i.e., to three years' detention in all, to be served in a corrective labor colony with an ordinary regime.

The rest of the verdict remains unchanged and the appeal is dismissed.*

Signatures

ROMANOV (Chairman)

KISELYOVA and YEVDOKIMENKO (Judges)

* The only practical difference is that Khaustov is to serve his sentence in a camp with an ordinary instead of a severe regime.

APPENDIX III

FINDINGS OF THE MOSCOW CITY COURT

on the 1st of September, 1967

The Judicial Collegium of the Moscow City Criminal Court, consisting of Chairman Yu. B. Shapovalova and People's Assessors P. D. Elfimov and L. N. Kireyeva, having—with the assistance of Clerk of the Court Makarova and the participation of Prosecutor V. M. Mironov and Defense Counsels D. I. Kaminskaya, N. S. Alsky and Sh. A. Melamed—heard in open court the case of:

Bukovsky, Vladimir Konstantinovich (born on the 30th of December, 1942, in the City of Belebey in the Bashkir Autonomous Soviet Socialist Republic, Russian, non-Party, unmarried, secondary education, unemployed, third category disabled, residing at 3/5 Furmanov Street, Flat 59, Moscow);

Delaunay, Vadim Nikolayevich (born on the 22nd of December, 1937, in the City of Moscow, Russian, non-Party, secondary education, working as a freelance correspondent of *Literary Gazette,* residing at 12 Pyatnitskaya Street, Flat 5, Moscow);

Kushev, Yevgeny Igorevich (born on the 3rd of August, 1947, in the City of Odessa, Russian, non-Party, unfinished secondary education, unemployed at time of arrest, residing at 10 Smolenskaya Street, Flat 174, Moscow)—

All three charged under Article 190/3 of the Criminal Code of the RSFSR—

finds that:

Accused Bukovsky, hearing of the arrest of his acquaintances Lashkova, Dobrovolsky, and others, and anxious to obtain their release, adopted—contrary to the established order for approaching the proper authorities —an illegal method of expressing his demands and his disagreement with Articles 70 and 190/1–3 of the Criminal Code of the RSFSR, acted as one of the organizers of group activities involving a grave breach of the peace in Pushkin Square in Moscow on the 22nd of January, 1967, and took an active part therein.

Bukovsky notified his acquaintances of the place, time, and purpose of the meeting, composed the text of the slogans "Release Dobrovolsky, Galanskov, Lashkova, and Radzievsky" and "We demand the revision of the anti-constitutional Decree and of Article 70 of the Criminal Code of the RSFSR," and himself manufactured one of the banners on which the slogans were inscribed. Among those whom Bukovsky notified were Defendants Delaunay and Kushev who took an active part in the proceedings.

On the 22nd of January, 1967, at 6:00 P.M. a large crowd gathered in Pushkin Square; Bukovsky and Delaunay held banners; Kushev shouted: "Release Dobrovolsky" and "Down with dictatorship."

Khaustov (since convicted), who was another organizer of these events and took an active part in them, refused to give up his banner to the *Druzhinniki,* who requested him to do so, and resisted them.

Bukovsky was therefore an organizer and an active participant, and Delaunay and Kushev were active participants in group activities involving a grave breach of the peace.

On being interrogated, Delaunay and Kushev admitted their guilt in full.

Bukovsky admitted the facts stated above but pleaded not guilty.

The charges are supported by the following evidence: statements by *Druzhinniki* Kleymenov, Dvoskin, Malakhov, and Cherkasov to the effect that, while they were on duty in connection with the maintenance of public order on the 22nd of January, a group of young people gathered near the Pushkin monument at 6 P.M., committed a grave breach of the peace, displayed three slogans demanding the release of prisoners Lashkova, Dobrovolsky, and others, and the revision of the Decree introducing Articles 190/1–3 and of Article 70 of the Criminal Code of the RSFSR; Kushev shouted: "Release Dobrovolsky" and "Down with dictatorship," Khaustov disobeyed the orders of the *Druzhinniki,* resisted arrest, and refused to give up his banner:

the evidence of witness Kucherova concerning the organization of the above activities, and the active role which Bukovsky played therein despite her efforts to dissuade him;

the evidence of witnesses Katz and Khaustov who were eyewitnesses of and participants in these events;

finally, the charges are also supported by the statements of the defendants themselves and by the material evidence in the case.

Having examined the evidence, the Judicial Collegium finds that the charges are proved.

In deciding the penalties to be imposed on each of the accused, the Judicial Collegium takes into account the more active and organizational role of Bukovsky; it also takes into account the sincere regret for this, their first offense, shown by Delaunay and Kushev, and considers it possible, by way of an exception and in view of the above-mentioned circumstances, to apply to Delaunay and Kushev the provisions of Article 44 of the Criminal Code of the RSFSR.

In view of the above-mentioned facts and in accordance with Articles 301, 303, and 315 of the Procedural Code of Criminal Law of the RSFSR, the Judicial Collegium of the Moscow City Criminal Court finds the defendants guilty under Articles 190/3 of the C.C. of the RSFSR, and sentences

Bukovsky, V. K., to detention for three years, the term to run as from the date of his arrest, the 26th of January, 1967, and to be served in a corrective labor colony with an ordinary regime;

Delaunay, V. N., and Kushev, Ye. I., to detention for one year each, the term to be served in a corrective labor camp with an ordinary regime.

In accordance with Article 44 of the Criminal Code of the RSFSR, the sentence passed on Delaunay and Kushev is to be suspended for five years.

Delaunay and Kushev are to be released.

The material evidence—three slogans—to be destroyed.

Bukovsky to be kept under guard.

Signed

YU. B. SHAPOVALOVA (Chairman)

P. D. ELFIMOV and L. N. KIREYEVA (People's Assessors)

APPENDIX IV

VERDICT OF THE SUPREME COURT OF THE RSFSR

16th of November, 1967

The Judicial Collegium of the Supreme Court of the RSFSR, consisting of Chairman I. M. Karashev and members of the Court K. E. Gavrilin and V. I. Yershov has, on the 16th of November, 1967, heard the appeal of Defense Counsel D. I. Kaminskaya against the sentence passed on V. K. Bukovsky by the Moscow City Court on the 1st of September, 1967, whereby

Bukovsky, Vladimir Konstantinovich (biographical

facts as on page 152), was sentenced, in accordance with Article 190/3 of the Criminal Code of the RSFSR, to detention for three years, a term to be served in a corrective labor colony with an ordinary regime.

Under the same article, his co-defendants, Delaunay and Kushev, received a suspended sentence of one year each in a corrective labor colony with an ordinary regime.

Having heard the report of Judge I. M. Karashev, the explanations of Defense Counsel D. I. Kaminskaya in support of her appeal, and the conclusions of Prosecutor V. M. Yakovlev, who submitted that the sentence should be left unchanged, the Judicial Collegium

found that:

Bukovsky was guilty of organizing activities involving a serious breach of the peace and of playing an active part therein.

The offense was committed in Pushkin Square in Moscow on the 22nd of January, 1967, in the following circumstances:

[description as on page 144]

At his trial Bukovsky pleaded not guilty.

In her appeal, Defense Counsel Kaminskaya requests that the sentence be quashed and the case dismissed for lack of evidence. She points out that, in organizing the demonstration, Bukovsky did not intend to commit a breach of the peace; and that Khaustov's resistance to arrest was an excess of zeal on the part of an executive, i.e., it does not constitute evidence of intent on Bukovsky's part.

On the above-mentioned grounds, Bukovsky also requests that the sentence be quashed and the case dismissed.

Having examined the evidence in the case and the arguments in support of the appeal, the Judicial Collegium finds the sentence to be valid.

Bukovsky's guilt is proved by the evidence which was carefully examined in the course of the trial.

Although Bukovsky pleaded not guilty, he did not deny, either during the preliminary investigation or at his trial, the fact that he had organized a large gathering in the Square with the purpose of publicly voicing the demands of his group for the revision of certain laws and the release of their acquaintances arrested and charged with anti-Soviet agitation and propaganda, for which purpose he had composed the text of the slogans and had himself manufactured one of the banners. Neither did he deny that he had taken an active part in the demonstration which he had organized.

Witness Kucherova confirmed that Bukovsky was one of the most active organizers of the group activities which took place in the Square, and that he persisted in this despite her efforts to dissuade him.

The evidence of witnesses Kleymenov, Dvoskin, Malakhov, and others shows that, while they were on duty in connection with the maintenance of public order on the 22nd of January, 1967, a large group of young people gathered at 6 P.M. in Pushkin Square, committed a grave breach of the peace, displayed three slogans with the above-mentioned texts; Kushev shouted, "Release

Dobrovolsky" and "Down with dictatorship," while Khaustov disobeyed the orders of the *Druzhinniki,* refused to give up his banner, and resisted arrest.

Bukovsky's guilt is also confirmed by the evidence of witnesses Katz (an active participant in the demonstration) and Khaustov (its active participant and co-organizer with Bukovsky); by the evidence of Delaunay and Kushev about the nature of the demonstration and Bukovsky's organizational role; and by the material evidence in the case.

Having weighed the evidence as a whole, the Moscow City Court rightly concluded that the activities of the group organized by Bukovsky had involved a grave breach of the peace in one of the populous squares of the City of Moscow, and rightly sentenced him under Article 190/3 of the C.C. of the RSFSR.

In view of the above, the appellants' argument, that Bukovsky had not intended to commit a breach of the peace, cannot be accepted as convincing and the appeal is dismissed.

Bukovsky's allegation that a breach of the provisions of Article 126 of the Procedural Code of Criminal Law of the RSFSR was committed in the course of the investigation, is found to be groundless.

As the records show, the case was started by the Moscow Prosecutor's Office on evidence of an offense against Article 190/3 of the C.C. of the RSFSR. As stated in the order referring the case to the Investigating Section of the Moscow and Moscow District KGB Department of the Council of Ministers of the USSR, facts established during the investigation proved the anti-social character of Bukovsky's and the other defendants' action.

The fact that the investigation by the KGB failed to produce evidence of an offense against Article 70 of the C.C. of the RSFSR does not prove that the provisions of Article 126 of the Procedural Code of the Criminal Code of the RSFSR were infringed.

In view of the above and in accordance with Article 339 of the Procedural Code of Criminal Law of the RSFSR, the Judicial Collegium holds that the sentence passed on Bukovsky by the Moscow City Court on the 1st of September, 1967, be left unchanged and the appeal be dismissed.

    Signed

I. B. KARASEV (Chairman)

K. E. GAVRILIN and V. I. YERSHOV (Judges)

APPENDIX V

ARTICLE 70   *Agitation or propaganda* carried out with the purpose of weakening or subverting the Soviet regime or of committing particularly dangerous crimes against the State, the dissemination for the said purposes of slanderous inventions discrediting the Soviet political and social system, as also the dissemination or production or harboring for the said purposes of literature of a similar content—is punishable by six months to seven years of detention with or without a further period of two to five years of exile, or by two to five years of exile.

ARTICLE 206/1   *Hooliganism,* i.e., deliberate actions involving a serious breach of the peace and clearly expressing disrespect for society—is punishable by two years of detention, or two years of corrective labor, or a fine of fifty rubles, or a public reprimand.

ARTICLE 206/2   *Malicious hooliganism,* i.e., similar actions committed by a person previously tried for hooliganism, or combined with resistance to a representative of authority or a representative of the public in the execution of his duty in maintaining public order, or distinguished by exceptional cynicism or insolence—is punishable by a term of up to five years of detention.

ARTICLE 191/1   [added to the C.C. by a Decree of the Supreme Soviet of the RSFSR on the 25th of July, 1962]

    i. *Resistance to members of the police or the Druzhinniki* in the execution of their duty of maintaining public order—is punishable by one year of detention, or one year of corrective labor or a fine up to one hundred rubles.

ii. Similar actions combined with the threat or the use of violence, as also actions compelling such persons by the threat or the use of violence to break the law—are punishable by one to five years' detention.

APPENDIX VI

LETTER BY P. GRIGORENKO

To: A. F. GORKIN, Chairman of the Supreme Court of the USSR, and R. A. RUDENKO, Prosecutor General of the USSR:

Our country and progressive people everywhere have just observed the 50th anniversary of the Great October Revolution.

Almost immediately after this, the 50th anniversary of Soviet law was observed. On that date our press published a series of articles in praise of Soviet law, asserting, in particular, that it is the most just, the most unbiased, and the most humane in the world.

My own experience literally cries out against these

assertions. Nevertheless, I have decided to base my assumptions on them and not on my personal experience. For that reason I am addressing this letter to you.

Not long ago, I learned that on February 16, 1967, the Moscow City Court sentenced a Moscow worker, Viktor Khaustov, to three years' deprivation of freedom under Article 190/3 of the Criminal Code of the RSFSR.

This article and two others (Articles 190/1 and 190/2) were enacted by the Presidium of the Supreme Soviet of the RSFSR in the name of "the struggle against hooliganism" and without the knowledge of the broad masses of the people.

One of these three articles—190/2*—has met with no objection whatever from Soviet public opinion. If acts of disrespect to the seal or the flag of the Soviet Union were being committed on a wide scale, this evil could obviously be suppressed by applying any one of several other existing legal measures.

The other two sections of Article 190 are a different matter. Upon learning that these provisions had been enacted into law, leading members of our society immediately stated that they made it possible to suppress liberties guaranteed under Article 125 of the Constitution of the USSR—freedom of speech, of the press, of assembly, meetings, and demonstration, as well as of the greatest weapon of the working class: freedom to strike.

However, competent authorities denied that such a

* Article 190/2 qualifies acts of disrespect to the flag or the seal of the Soviet Union as specific crimes.

possibility existed. They stated that there was no question of suppressing the above-mentioned freedoms, but rather of making sure that they were not used for the purpose of venomously slandering Soviet society and the Soviet political structure, or for the violation of public order, or for the disruption of the work of industrial enterprises, transport, government offices, and institutions.

The trial of Khaustov showed how flimsy these explanations were. Even in the highly charged atmosphere of the courtroom, it was established beyond any doubt that Khaustov took part in a very small, peaceful demonstration during which there was no breach of the peace and no obstruction of the movement of public transport or of passers-by, or of the work of State or public enterprises, offices, and institutions.

Furthermore, in their anxiety to avoid disorder of any kind, the demonstrators offered no resistance even when they were exposed to an unprovoked hooligan attack. That the attack was hooligan in character was made perfectly plain. How else can one describe an incident in which unknown people hurl themselves without any warning upon peaceful demonstrators and commit outrages of physical violence? The fact as established at the trial that the attackers were members of the Komsomol Operational Squad and employees of the KGB, so far from making the attack legitimate, makes it even more bestial. Why indeed was it necessary to break up the demonstration by using KGB personnel in civilian clothes and members of the Komsomol Operational

Squad without armbands? Why was it necessary to attack and to use physical force instead of peacefully asking the demonstrators to disperse?

You will agree that the attack can best be described as a provocation. It looks as if its purpose was to provoke the demonstrators to resist, so that, later on, a big trial of "hooligans" could be organized. The fact that the uniformed police and, later, the Court, sided with the attackers goes to prove this supposition.

All the evidence produced at the trial went to show that the accused had not committed a crime. In spite of this he was charged under the above-mentioned Articles of the Criminal Code. The Court did not even note that Khaustov had no previous criminal record, that upon finishing high school he began working in a factory and continued to do so honestly for ten years, or that he is the only breadwinner in his family.

We can only conclude that the trial was a political one. Khaustov was convicted not for disturbing public order, but because he held certain personal views on current events and because he did not keep silent when he saw responsible representatives of authority supressing the legal rights of Soviet citizens. More specifically, he was tried for organizing, conducting and participating in a demonstration of protest against illegal arrests.

The political character of this trial was exposed with even greater force when, in September, 1967, three other men who had taken part in this very demonstration— Bukovsky, Delaunay, and Kushev—were brought to trial after seven months' detention in the investigation prison of the KGB. The authorities were unable even to bring forth the ludicrous accusation they had brought against Khaustov, namely that he had hit someone with the pole of the wooden placard which the attackers were trying to pull away from him.

This time, everything was different. Delaunay and Kushev had offered no resistance whatsoever and had gone to the police station as soon as they were requested to do so. Bukovsky, indeed, behaved in such a way that the attackers failed even to notice him. Despite the fact that he left the square later than any of the other demonstrators, no one had so much as tried to detain him. In a completely senseless and ridiculous fashion, he was arrested a week later at his flat, and charged under Article 190/3. Obviously, a man cannot hide a breach of the peace which he has already committed in the drawers of his desk or between the pages of a book.

Like the trial of Khaustov, that of Bukovsky and his two comrades was, in practice, conducted behind closed doors, and accompanied by outrageous violations of the rights of the accused. By his many interjections and warnings, as well as by calling a recess before Bukovsky had finished his final statement, the judge prevented the accused from exercising his right to defend himself. The Court paid no attention to Bukovsky's statement (though it was not refuted by anyone) concerning the crude violations of legality which had taken place during the pre-trial investigation.

As for the sentence! For the very same actions for which the Court sentenced Bukovsky to the highest penalty provided by the law—three years in a forced labor camp—his two comrades were only put on probation. One naturally asks, why? The whole course of the trial shows the reason and leaves no doubt in one's mind. Bukovsky was sentenced because he defended himself, and because he refused to recognize the right of the KGB to engage in uncontrolled and illegal interference in the personal lives of citizens. Delaunay and Kushev were "encouraged" to "express remorse" even though they had not committed any criminal act.

Proceeding from the above, as a citizen of my country, entitled to all its rights and in duty bound to observe unswervingly its basic law, the Soviet Constitution, I demand that the Supreme Court of the USSR:

review the cases of Khaustov, Bukovsky, Delaunay, and Kushev, remit the illegal sentences, and release the accused;

explain to all the lower courts that participation in gatherings, meetings, demonstrations, and strikes is not to be tried under Article 190/3, and that only genuine breaches of the peace should be tried;

use the cases cited by me as precedents to show that in these given instances the disturbers of public order were not the demonstrators but those who attacked them;

publish these judicial commentaries, not merely in technical legal publications but in the mass circulation press.

Obviously, if statements to the effect that Soviet law is unbiased, just, and humane are to have any real worth whatsoever; if Article 112 of the Constitution of the USSR, which says that judges are independent and responsible only to the law, has any meaning, the Supreme Court must put into effect the basic law of the socialist state, remit the illegal sentences, and take measures to prevent anything of the sort happening in the future.

If it fails to do so, it will be clear that the Supreme Court, as one of the basic organs of power, is taking a direct part in the attack on the constitutional rights of citizens and covering up its actions with lofty words about justice, impartiality, and humanitarianism. In such an eventuality, citizens would have a right to defend the Constitution by all available means—above all, by the full exposure of the anti-constitutional acts of government organs, including the illegal sentences passed by the courts.

P. GRIGORENKO

December, 1967
Piotr Grigorevich Grigorenko
Moscow, G-21, Komsomolsky Prospekt
Building 14/1, Flat 96, Telephone G6-27-37

(English text published in *Problems of Communism,* vol. 17.)

NOTE ON GENERAL GRIGORENKO

Pyotr (or Peter) Grigorenko, now in his sixties, rose to the rank of Major General in the war, was several times wounded, and afterward became a teacher of cybernetics at the prestigious Frunze Military Academy in Moscow. In 1961 he was transferred to the Far East for criticizing Khrushchev's policies on military and political matters, and then in 1964, although quite sane, imprisoned in a mental hospital, deprived of his rank, and expelled from the Party. A year later he was released and soon became one of the leaders of the Soviet civil rights movement. He protested at injustices, tried to attend political trials, and championed the persecuted Crimean Tatars—all within the framework of Soviet law. On May 7, 1969, he was at last arrested in Tashkent.

NOTES

NOTES

1   RSFSR: Russian Soviet Federal Socialist Republic, of which the capital is Moscow and which is the largest of the constituent republics of the USSR.

2   Article 70 (for full text, see Appendix V) imposes penalties of up to seven years of detention followed by five of exile for "propaganda . . . aimed at undermining or weakening the Soviet regime." Sinyavsky and Daniel were sentenced under this article in February, 1966, when, for the first time, it was used against writers for their works of fiction. The trial was followed by a wave of protests and demonstrations against the verdict and Article 70. The Government reacted by passing the Decree introducing Articles 190/1–3 and arresting a number of demonstrators.

3   The Russian term used throughout the text is *zaderzhali:* "detained." Police and investigators are empowered to detain a person if they have reasonable grounds to suspect him of a crime. But the Prosecutor (see Note 7) must be informed within twenty-four hours and he, within another forty-eight, must decide whether to sanction the detention or release the suspect. In the former instance, detention becomes arrest.

4   Members of the Komsomol (Young Communist League) are enrolled into Operational Squads, also called *Druzhiny* ("brigades"), to act as volunteers assisting the police.

5   KGB: "Committee of State Security"—Security Service.

6   *Samizdat:* "self-publication"—current term for unpublished manuscripts circulated privately.

7   The Bench in a Soviet court consists of a Chairman (a judge, who is a trained lawyer, elected for five years) and

two People's Assessors (*narodnyie zasidateli*), laymen elected for a fortnight a year for two years to fulfill functions theoretically similar to those of the jury in a Western court; the difference is that they have the right to intervene in the proceedings in the same way as the judge. Judge and lay assessors decide all questions, including the verdict, by a majority vote.

The Clerk is merely a secretary who keeps the record of the proceedings.

The Prosecutor (*prokurator*) combines the functions of the French Juge d'Instruction with that of the French parquet. Perhaps the nearest equivalent in the U.K. is the Prosecutor Fiscal in Scotland. His office (*prokuratura*) conducts the pre-trial investigation (*predvaritelnoye sledstviye*), unless the nature of the offense brings it within the competence of the KGB.

8   For full text of Article 206, see Appendix V. The Articles (throughout the text) are those of the Criminal Code of the RSFSR. Soviet criminal and civil law falls under the jurisdiction of the fifteen constituent Republics, each of which legislates its own code. These fifteen codes vary only slightly, because all conform to general principles established by the Central, All-Union Government. These federal principles, known as "Fundamentals," settle all major problems of criminal theory and outline the law in considerable detail: the Republics are left to fill the gaps and adjust to local peculiarities. The current Fundamentals were enacted by the Supreme Soviet of the USSR in 1958; the Russian Code by the Supreme Soviet of the RSFSR in 1960.

9   *Druzhinniki*: Members of *Druzhiny*. See Note 4.

10 The 5th of December is "Constitution Day." A demonstration demanding an open trial for Sinyavsky and Daniel was held on that date in 1965, and one against attempts at rehabilitating Stalin in 1966.

11 *Phoenix*: one of a series of underground literary periodicals. The first in recent years was the poetry periodical *Syntaxis,* suppressed in 1960 when the editor, A. Ginzburg, and others were arrested. *Phoenix* appeared in 1965 and 1966; extracts were published in the West.

12 For text of Article on Hooliganism, see Appendix V.

13 A sentence to *lisheniye svobody* ("deprivation of freedom")

is rarely served in prison (*tyurma*), which is reserved for "especially serious crimes" and "especially dangerous recidivists." The more usual places of detention are corrective labor camps (now known as "colonies") which are of four kinds: the "regime" (discipline, etc.) may be *obschchy* ("ordinary" or "general"), *usilenny* ("severe" or "reinforced"), *strogy* ("very severe") or *spetsidalny* ("special"). Those with an "ordinary" regime are mainly for first offenders and petty crimes; those with a "special" regime are for dangerous recidivists. Food, punishments, number of letters, parcels, and visits allowed, etc., vary according to the category.

14 For text of Article on resistance to authorities, see Appendix V.

15 NTS (*Narodno-trudovoy soyuz*—"People's Labor Alliance"): a Russian émigré anti-Communist organization.

16 SMOG (*Samoye Molodoye Obshchestvo Geniyev*—"The Youngest Society of Geniuses" as these young people called themselves): a group of young writers and poets, mostly undergraduates, who published an underground periodical and were involved in a demonstration for freedom of art in April, 1965, and another, demanding an open trial for Sinyavsky and Daniel, in December of that year.

17 Cult of Personality—official euphemism for Stalin's dictatorship.

18 *Bell* (*Kolokol*): originally the name of the 19th-century revolutionary periodical published by Alexander Herzen in London.

19 Union of Soviet Writers founded in 1932 to which the great majority of professional Soviet writers belong. Membership involves a number of material and other privileges, while expulsion makes it impossible to be published. Backed by the Government, it represents the literary establishment and its Board implements the Government's literary policy.

20 Many factories have literary study and discussion groups.

21 "Social parasite" (*tuneyadets*), i.e., a person who does no socially useful work, is a Soviet legal term.

22 Venyamin Kaverin (born 1902): well-known novelist and short-story writer.

23 A collection of Krasnov's theological articles was published in the West.

24 K. F. Ryleyev (1795–1826): poet executed as one of the leaders of the Decembrist uprising against Nicholas I.

25 "Peoples' Will": a revolutionary organization founded in 1879 and broken up by the police in the 1880's.

26 Translator of Dickens and other English authors; daughter of Maxim Litvinov, who was Foreign Secretary, then Ambassador, to Washington under Stalin; aunt of Pavel Litvinov.

27 Alexander Yesenin-Volpin: mathematician, philosopher, and poet; son of the famous poet Sergei Yesenin, who committed suicide in 1926.

28 His poems and a philosophical essay, unpublished in the USSR, appeared in the West.

29 Babi Yar: scene of a Nazi massacre of the Jews during the war, later turned into a park of culture and rest; no monument was put up to mark the mass grave, as Yevtushenko noted in his famous poem against anti-Semitism.

30 The two Soviet national holidays—the 7th of November, anniversary of the October Revolution, and the 1st of May—when the parade in Red Square is followed by processions of citizens organized by trade unions and other official bodies.

31 Bezobrazov: the name is derived from the Russian word for "disgrace": *bezobrazie.*

32 For full text of letter, see Appendix VI.